PARIS JAZZ

PARIS JAZZ
A GUIDE

FROM THE JAZZ AGE TO THE PRESENT

LUKE MINER

THE LITTLE BOOKROOM · NEW YORK

© 2005 Luke Miner

Book Design: Louise Fili Ltd.

Every attempt has been made to ensure the accuracy of the information
in this book. We strongly suggest that you call the establishments in
advance to ensure that opening days and hours have not changed.

Library of Congress Cataloging-in-Publication Data

Miner, Luke, 1978 —
Paris jazz : from the jazz age to the present : a guide / Luke Miner.
p. cm.
ISBN 1-892145-29-4
1. Jazz—France—Paris—History and criticism. 2. Musical landmarks—France—Paris—Guidebooks.
3. Paris (France)—Guidebooks. I. Title.
ML3509.F7M56 2005
781.65'0944'361—dc22
2004025927
ISBN-13 : 978-1-892145-29-1
ISBN 10 : 1-892145-29-1

Published by The Little Bookroom
1755 Broadway, Fifth floor, New York, NY 10019
phone (212) 293-1643, fax (212) 333-5374
www.littlebookroom.com

Manufactured in China by P. Chan & Edward, Inc.
1 3 5 7 9 10 8 6 4 2

contents

introduction

PARIS'S FIRST JAZZ MUSICIANS ARRIVED NEAR THE END OF WORLD WAR I, AND, APART FROM A BRIEF PAUSE DURING WORLD WAR II, they continued to come in successive waves well into the 1960s. Some, like Josephine Baker, were lured by tales of Paris's glitz and glamour, while others, like Sidney Bechet, were drawn by greater pay and work opportunities. Almost all African-American jazz musicians visiting Paris were struck by the city's relative racial tolerance. After a tour through Europe in 1939, Duke Ellington famously said: "You can go anywhere and talk to anybody and do anything you like. It's hard to believe. When you've eaten hot dogs all your life and you're suddenly offered caviar it's hard to believe it's true."

Jazz emerged in New Orleans at the end of the nineteenth century out of a confluence of African and European music, but didn't gain widespread appreciation as an art form until the birth of Dixieland in the late teens. By the time Josephine Baker had made her debut at the Pariss Theatre, jazz had become a dominant force in American life with artists such as Louis Armstrong, Kid Ory, and Joe "King" Oliver playing in cities from Kansas City to New York. Up until the sixties, Paris was the main center for jazz outside of America, and followed closely behind New York in adopting the latest styles and sounds. It wasn't until the seventies, when jazz became more international, that Paris developed a significant number of native jazz musicians and became a jazz force in its own right.

France's first jazz musicians arrived at a time when Paris was the cultural capital of Europe, and the home of Picasso, Stravinsky, Hemingway, Fitzgerald, and Modigliani, among others. Rather than being lost among this crush of painters, composers, and writers, these jazz expatriates carved a niche of their own, influencing not only contemporary Parisian society, but the shape and direction of French culture as well. Composer Erik Satie wove jazz- and ragtime-inflected passages into some of his more famous pieces, Matisse named a book of cutouts after jazz, and the director Louis Malle commissioned Miles Davis to compose the soundtrack for one of his first films, *Ascenseur pour l'échafaud.* Jazz has since joined the opera and ballet as a national institution, with a French national jazz orchestra since 1986, and a jazz department at Paris's prestigious Conservatoire National Supérieur de Musique since 1992.

If jazz has had a profound effect upon French culture, France has had an equally significant impact on jazz. As early as the 1930s, jazz appreciation societies sprouted up all over France, providing some of the first serious criticism of the burgeoning art form. With the emergence of Django Reinhardt and Stéphane Grappelli in France, jazz musicians in America encountered some of their first real international competition. Reinhardt's distinct gypsy-influenced playing style would lead to the birth of a new subset of jazz, called jazz *manouche* (gypsy jazz). Even today, French musicians continue to innovate, adding not only Gallic sounds to the jazz mixture, but African and Berber influences as well.

To many embittered by the First World War, American popular culture represented a refreshing break from the past. During the twenties, American popular culture swept through French society, introducing Hollywood films with Mae West and Charlie Chaplin into theaters once dominated by France's native film industry; filling newspapers with American comic strips like Donald Duck, Dick Tracy, and Flash Gordon; and replacing traditional French music with jazz.

This book introduces Paris's jazz community and the indelible effect it has had on the city. It proceeds in near-chronological order through some of Paris's most famous neighborhoods, to the homes, clubs, bars, and music halls responsible for the spread of jazz over the past century:

- MONTMARTRE, which welcomed jazz musicians at the end of World War I
- MONTPARNASSE, where France's first native jazz musicians mixed with the American expatriate community
- The area around the CHAMPS-ÉLYSÉES, where Josephine Baker and, later, Dizzy Gillespie made their explosive debuts
- SAINT-GERMAIN-DES-PRÉS, where Sartre's existentialist circle packed into small subterranean clubs to experience cutting-edge bebop

Parisians are proud of their cultural heritage and most of the stops mentioned in this book have been well preserved. All of the stops can be located on the map accompanying each chapter.

This book explores Paris's rich jazz history at both its most spectacular and its most sordid. Following the footsteps of the music's first emissaries can reveal aspects of the city that even the seasoned native may have overlooked. In the process, one is likely to discover that, eighty years after first arriving on French soil, jazz music is more influential than ever.

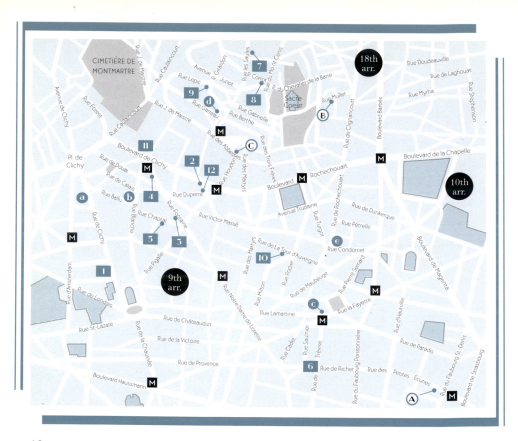

MONTMARTRE

1 CASINO DE PARIS

2 SITE OF THE GRAND DUC

3 SITE OF BRICKTOP'S

4 SITE OF CHEZ JOSEPHINE'S

5 SITE OF HOT CLUB DE FRANCE

6 FOLIES-BERGÈRE   7 LAPIN AGILE

8 MUSÉE LE PLACARD D'ERIK SATIE

9 MOULIN DE LA GALETTE

10 FORMER RESIDENCE OF LOUIS ARMSTRONG

11 MOULIN ROUGE

12 SITE OF THE BIG APPLE

a FORMER RESIDENCE OF LOUIS MITCHELL

b SITE OF THE MUSIC BOX   c FORMER RESIDENCE OF STÉPHANE GRAPPELLI

d BÂTEAU LAVOIR   e FORMER RESIDENCE OF STÉPHANE GRAPPELLI

A NEW MORNING   B LE BLUE NOTE   C HOUDON

M METRO STOP

MONTMARTRE

MONTMARTRE IS A DENSE COLLECTION OF STREETS AND ALLEYS THAT WIND ALONG THE SIDE OF PARIS'S TALLEST HILL, LA BUTTE, before climbing to meet at the basilica of Sacré-Coeur. In 1900, the quarter was one of the most unsavory areas of Paris, where prostitutes and drug dealers regularly plied their trades. Its inexpensive rents and impressive city views also made it a center of bohemian society long before the arrival of jazz. Over the course of a half-century, Montmartre played host to the realists, impressionists, postimpressionists, and Picasso's circle of painters. But while Paris's struggling artists favored the picturesque roads and alleys at the hill's top, jazz musicians preferred to congregate around the seedy boulevards and squares at La Butte's base, establishing a small section of Harlem in Paris.

Paris's first jazz messengers arrived at the tail end of World War I with Louis Mitchell's Jazz Kings in Paris and James Reese Europe's Hellfighters in the provinces. Europe's Hellfighters was an all-African-American ragtime marching band drawn from the members of New York's 15th Infantry. A towering figure of early jazz, Europe had gained his fame by founding the Clef Club, an influential musician's guild in New York, and by leading one of the first all-black orchestras. Apart from Europe, the Hellfighters featured many other important artists, including Noble Sissle, who later wrote the classic musical *Shuffle Along*, and Bill "Bojangles" Robinson, a Broadway dancer who went on to perform in fourteen movies. Besides their musical success, the infantry also earned distinction on the battlefield, becoming the first American unit to reach the Rhine and earning the French Croix de Guerre for its efforts.

In what would become a familiar observation for African-Americans in France, these band-members were amazed by the lack of racism among the French. Rather than being treated like inferiors, they were celebrated for their talent and "exotic" looks. When faced with the daunting prospect of returning to a still segregated America, many of these musicians decided to stay, forming the first core group of jazz expatriates in Paris.

Over the course of the next two decades, these musicians would make an enduring impression upon their new home, transforming Montmartre into the heart of France's jazz age. Lasting from the early twenties until the end of the thirties, the jazz age permanently transformed French society. For the first time, artists of different social and racial backgrounds—Jean Cocteau, Ernest Hemingway, Josephine Baker, Langston Hughes—floated in similar circles. This mixing was extremely fertile for the arts, imbuing movements like Dadaism, surrealism, and futurism with jazz undertones.

Paris's warm embrace of the jazz age was encouraged by the cultural climate. Having just won a war costing millions of lives, France was ready to leave the past behind and celebrate. With its many music halls, cabarets, and night clubs already in place, Montmartre and its environs became the natural destination for Parisian revelers eager to experience the new sounds and steps of jazz.

Although Montmartre's jazz scene continued to grow after the war, it wasn't until Josephine Baker's arrival in 1925 as a member of *La Revue Nègre* that jazz leapt from the back streets of La Butte into mainstream French society. Baker's sexual charm took the country by storm, transforming jazz culture from a mere curiosity into a vogue. By the end of the decade some of America's finest musicians such as Duke Ellington, Buddy Gilmore, and Sidney Bechet would make their way through the winding streets of Montmartre, turning it into the jazz capital of Europe and a rival of Harlem.

James Reese Europe conducting the Hellfighters, 1918. National Archives

casíno de parís

16 RUE DE CLICHY · PHONE: 08.92.69.89.26 · MÉTRO: LIÈGE/TRINITÉ
WWW.CASINODEPARIS.FR · OPEN DAILY: 8:30PM–11:30PM

CONVERTED IN THE 1880S FROM AN ICE-SKATING RINK INTO A MUSIC HALL, THE CASINO DE PARIS WAS DECORATED IN AN EASTERN theme, featuring exotic rooms such as the "Indian Salon," where large red globes hung from the ceiling to illuminate rows of delicately gilded columns. In another chamber known as "Mahomet's Paradise," men in turbans and trousers rested immobile against a wall, waiting for a tap on the belly and a few centimes in the hand to entertain the curious guest.

In 1918, the Casino de Paris opened its doors to Paris's first jazz band, Louis Mitchell's Jazz Kings. Although the band's sound had little in common with what is now considered jazz, its syncopated beats and improvised solos were so new and foreign that it immediately took the city by storm. Poet and film director Jean Cocteau described Mitchell as "a barman of noises under a gilt pergola loaded with bells, triangles, boards, and motorcycle horns," and concluded: "the house was on its feet to applaud, roused from its inertia by this extraordinary turn, which compared to the madness of Offenbach, is what a tank would be to an 1870 State Carriage." Soon after the arrival of the Jazz Kings, similar outfits opened in music halls all around Paris. However, the French were very new to jazz and their first attempts—featuring bells, Klaxons, and sometimes even revolvers—sounded more like an indistinguishable wall of noise than a well-trained band.

Louis Mitchell settled at 69 rue de Clichy ⓐ with his wife and son shortly after arriving in Paris. His apartment would become one of the city's first informal African-American salons, where decommissioned soldiers rubbed elbows with up-and-coming musicians, while Mitchell sat back and gave advice on how to succeed in Paris. His Jazz Kings would stay at the Casino de Paris until 1923, backing up famous dance hall performers like Mistinguett and Chevalier. Following the dissolution of the Jazz Kings, Mitchell went on to open his own club in Montmartre.

Unlike Paris's two more famous music halls, the Moulin Rouge and the Folies-Bergère, the Casino de Paris has opened its doors to a wide range of performances, including jazz concerts, comedy shows, and musicals. Possibly as a result of this shift, the locale is slightly less showy than its counterparts, providing simple yet elegant seats, housed under a roof crossed with gold squares.

19

site of the grand duc

52 RUE PIGALLE

BEFORE EUGENE BULLARD OPENED THE GRAND DUC IN 1924, THERE WAS NO OFFICIAL HOME FOR THE GROWING COMMUNITY OF AFRICAN-American musicians in Paris. And yet by the end of that decade, the Grand Duc had become the place where newly arrived musicians could find work and even a springboard for many of the era's great talents.

Bullard ascended to the heights of Parisian society from modest beginnings. Born the grandson of slaves in Columbus, Georgia, in 1894, he was chased out of his hometown at the age of seven by a lynch mob. Having heard stories of France's racial tolerance, he decided to make his way to Paris, stowing away on a freighter headed for Germany when he was only ten. It would take him another nine years, but he finally reached Paris in 1913 after a brief stint as a boxer in Britain. When the war broke out he fought in the French Foreign Legion, serving first as an infantryman in the battle of Verdun and later as an ace fighter pilot, where his exploits earned him the nickname "Black Swallow of Death." By the time the war had ended, Bullard had transformed himself yet again, learning the drums so that he could participate in Paris's burgeoning jazz culture.

For African-Americans, the Grand Duc was a hub where people met between gigs to receive messages, exchange gossip, and listen to stories from New York. Some nights, after the crowds had left, off-duty jazz musicians held impromptu jam sessions lasting well into the next day, stopping only to eat Bullard's down-home American fare: corned-beef hash with a poached egg, creamed chicken on toast, and club sandwiches. When writer Langston Hughes came to Paris in the winter of 1924, he had seven dollars in his pocket, no job prospects, and no place to stay. He managed to scrape by on this paltry sum for several weeks before finally landing a job at the Grand Duc as a dishwasher, backup cook, and waiter during the spring and summer of 1924. He described it as a place where "the cream of the Negro musicians then in France...would weave out music that would almost make your heart stand still at dawn....Blues in the rue Pigalle. Black and laughing, heart-breaking blues in the Paris dawn, pounding like a pulse-beat, moving like the Mississippi!"

Although wildly popular during the twenties, the Grand Duc was surprisingly run-down. One account describes it as "about twelve tables and a small bar that would feel crowded with six pairs of elbows leaning on it." Despite its shabbiness, the club enjoyed a distinguished clientele. It was a place where prostitutes and Corsican pimps fraternized with rich and famous guests like the Prince of Wales, Fatty Arbuckle, Charlie Chaplin, F. Scott Fitzgerald, Gloria Swanson, and Cole Porter.

Celebrated guests aside, the Grand Duc could be dangerous. The Corsican mafia that ran the neighborhood regularly demanded protection money from club owners, and Eugene Bullard once ended up in the hospital with a gunshot wound after a fight with a gangster. In his memoirs, Langston Hughes writes of several violent outbursts, including an especially fierce brawl that overwhelmed the entire establishment and forced Hughes to retreat to the top of the icebox.

Much of the Grand Duc's popularity can be attributed to Bricktop (Ada Louise Smith), an African-American singer and dancer who, along with Josephine Baker, ruled Parisian nightlife during the twenties. Although the Grand Duc would later propel Bricktop to great success within the Parisian cabaret scene, when she first laid eyes upon it she was so shocked by its raggedness that she broke down crying: "Do you mean to say this is the whole place? Have I come to Paris to entertain in a bar about the size of Connie's Inn? I had a twelve-piece band backing me up in New

York." Had it not been for Langston Hughes, who offered her a warm meal from the kitchen, she may have gone directly back to Harlem.

Today, a Chinese restaurant occupies the site of the Grand Duc.

site of bricktop's

SCOTT FITZGERALD ONCE SAID: "MY GREATEST CLAIM TO FAME IS THAT I DISCOVERED BRICKTOP BEFORE COLE PORTER." FITZGERALD happened upon the young entertainer by chance in 1925 and was so impressed that he became a regular at her club. Bricktop's even makes an appearance in Fitzgerald's "Babylon Revisited," a partially autobiographical account of his dissolute Parisian existence: "He passed a lighted door from which issued music, and stopped with the sense of familiarity; it was Bricktop's, where he had parted with so many hours and so much money." Fitzgerald wasn't her only admirer. Bricktop was a force in Montmartre's nightlife, bringing the best of Harlem jazz to Paris while courting a distinguished cast of international celebrities.

Born Ada Louise Smith in West Virginia in 1894, Bricktop earned her nickname because of her red hair and freckles. Her family moved to Chicago soon after her birth, where she grew up watching some of the era's premier black entertainers. At the age of sixteen, she joined a vaudeville troupe, spending the next few years

24

traveling around the United States before moving to Paris in 1924.

Considering the number of celebrities who visited Bricktop's in the twenties, the venue was surprisingly small. Benches and tables hugged the walls. The bottom-lit dance floor bathed the room in a sumptuous light. Bricktop would often leave the stage to walk among the audience, occasionally pausing to exchange a quip, rub a bald head, or dance with a guest. When she wasn't performing, Bricktop worked hard to keep her club up-to-date with the latest jazz from New York. During the twenties and thirties, she booked some of Paris's most innovative and exciting musicians, including Sidney Bechet, Buddy Gillmore, Cricket Smith, Django Reinhardt, and Stéphane Grappelli.

Bricktop gained access to the upper echelons of high society primarily through her knowledge of the Charleston. The dance took Paris by storm in 1925 after Josephine Baker's appearance in *La Revue Nègre* and soon became a sign of modernity among the city's youth, who had tired of older steps like the waltz and the java. Cole Porter was so taken by Bricktop's performance at the Grand Duc that he started throwing Charleston parties in his Left Bank mansion featuring Bricktop as both entertainer and dance teacher. By the end of the twenties, Bricktop was booked weeks in advance.

In her memoirs, she writes: "the shyest would-be Charleston dancer was the Aga Khan [the spiritual leader of a Shiite sect], and who wouldn't be, at over three hundred pounds...He never managed to ask me personally for Charleston lessons. The Marquise de Polignac was the one who told me that the Aga wanted to learn the Charleston...I was really sorry when he backed out of the lessons. He sent his driver with a very nice note calling the appointment off."

In her memoirs, Bricktop also recalls her friendship with F. Scott Fitzgerald, whom she described as a "little boy in a man's body. He hadn't grown up and didn't intend to and I liked that...When Scott got drunk, he was never mean or malicious. He just got more playful." Fitzgerald's drunken sprees sometimes turned destructive, however. Bricktop tells of one occasion when the police dropped Fitzgerald off at her club after catching him playing in the fountain of the Lido cabaret. Bricktop tried to send him back home in a cab, but to no avail. Ten minutes later he reappeared in the company of an angry taxi driver, having kicked out all the windows of the car. Fortunately, Fitzgerald always carried large rolls of money on him, so Bricktop was able to pay the man off. It wouldn't be the last time—according to Bricktop, she escorted Fitzgerald home three to four times a week.

One of Bricktop's earlier clubs, the Music Box, at 61 rue Blanche **ⓑ**, was the site of a now legendary confrontation. In a scene that was described by a witness as something "straight out of a cowboy movie," a skirmish between Sidney Bechet and a banjo player named Mike McKendrick erupted into a full-fledged gunfight on the sidewalk outside the club. Although the cause was benign—a passing comment about Bechet's failure to recognize a chord—the results were not: a pianist was shot in the leg, a dancer received a punctured lung, and a passerby was hit in the neck by a ricocheting bullet. Neither Bechet nor McKendrick suffered any injuries, although a bullet was lodged deep within Bechet's clothes. Years later, he claimed the stiffness of his collar was the only thing that had saved him from death. Both musicians served a year in prison and were then deported. Bechet did not return for another twenty years.

site of chez josephine's

39 RUE FONTAINE

JOSEPHINE BAKER OPENED HER OWN MONTMARTRE CLUB FOR A BRIEF TIME DURING THE LATE TWENTIES. UNLIKE BRICKTOP, BAKER catered exclusively to rich clientele, and it was not unusual to see heiresses at her club cavorting over tables of fantastically expensive champagne and caviar. Sometimes Baker would come out into the audience, pulling a beard and rubbing a belly before ushering everyone onto the dance floor. Other times she could be seen at the back of the room feeding her goat Toutoute and her pig Albert. The acclaimed Belgian crime novelist Georges Simenon worked at Chez Josephine's for a spell and almost edited a publication for her entitled *Josephine Baker's Magazine*. An infamous womanizer who claimed to have slept with more than five thousand women, Simenon also had an affair with Baker. When later asked why he didn't run off with her, he stated: "I was very poor at this time…and I did not want to be Mr. Baker."

síte of hot club de france

15 RUE CHAPTAL

JAZZ AFICIONADOS HUGH PANASSIÉ AND CHARLES DELAUNAY CRE-ATED THE HOT CLUB DE FRANCE AT 14 RUE CHAPTAL IN 1932 AS A means of diffusing jazz throughout the country. Over the next quarter-century, the organization transformed France's musical landscape, creating the country's most famous jazz band (the Quintette du Hot Club de France), and one of its first jazz magazines (*Jazz Hot*). It also staged numerous concerts and festivals that brought some of America's foremost jazz figures to Europe. The Hot Club even held regular lectures in which speakers like Hugh Panassié analyzed recordings measure by measure. Unlike in America, where jazz was strictly for dancing, in France it quickly became a near-academic pursuit.

Although the founders of the Hot Club de France shared a love of jazz, their approaches to the art form were strikingly different. Hugh Panassié first discovered jazz in 1926 when he took saxophone lessons from a musician in Josephine Baker's orchestra. Having inherited a large sum of money from his father, he was free to dedicate the rest of his life to the promotion and promulgation of jazz. In 1934 he wrote one of the first non-American books on jazz, entitled *Jazz Hot*, and would remain a firm devotee of traditional jazz for the rest of his life, rejecting bebop when it came into fashion in the late forties.

Son of the painters Robert and Sonia Delaunay, Charles Delaunay came from a sophisticated artistic background and, unlike Hugh Panassié, remained open to new sounds throughout his life. Delaunay was the ruling force behind the magazine *Jazz Hot* for several decades, and was enormously influential in French jazz until his death. In 1936, he wrote the first detailed list of jazz recordings, called "Hot Discography," marking the first use of the term "discography" (a comprehensive list of musical works).

Despite its initial success, the Hot Club de France was eventually split by a conflict between the two men that led to its permanent decline. At the end of World War II, the new and more challenging sounds of bebop began to filter into France through American GIs. Although Delaunay was delighted with the new music, Panassié considered bebop pretentious and self-indulgent. When it became clear to him that Delaunay planned to promote bebop through *Jazz Hot*, Panassié decided to make his move. He staged a coup d'état at the Hot Club's national conference, using his significant influence among the provincial chapters to eject Delaunay from the organization. As a consequence, the Hot Club de France was rent in two at the height of its powers, with the Paris chapter and *Jazz Hot* remaining faithful to Delaunay, and most of the provincial chapters standing by Panassié.

The Hot Club de France has long since declined in popularity, with little remaining but a few of Panassié's chapters. Current members are known for their encyclopedic knowledge of traditional jazz. For most jazz lovers the organization's website (www.hot-club.asso.fr) is an exercise in humility, featuring a quiz with questions like: "True or False? Jackie Davis recorded two titles for a 45 on the Victor label in 1941."

6

folíes-bergère

32 RUE DE RICHER · PHONE: 01.44.79.98.99 · MÉTRO: CADET
WWW.FOLIESBERGERE.COM · TUES–FRI: 8:30PM; SAT & SUN: 3:30PM

JOSEPHINE BAKER'S ROLE IN *LA REVUE NÈGRE* MAY HAVE MADE HER INTO A SENSATION, BUT HER PERFORMANCES AT THE FAMOUS Folies-Bergère music hall made her into a star. Only a year after appearing in a show entitled *La Folie du Jour* she commanded a passionate following and even released her own line of dolls, perfumes, pomades, and clothes.

Paris's first music hall, the Folies-Bergère opened in 1869 and over the years featured many celebrities including Charlie Chaplin, Maurice Chevalier, and Mistinguett. The Folies-Bergère possessed the aura of an extravagant Turkish bath with ceilings crossed with tassels of red and brown, vast floors covered with with tables and divans, and its fountains decorated with nudes, ferns, and enormous bronze saucers. Despite its chic reputation and distinguished clientele, it was not immune to the seedy side of Parisian nightlife. In order to reach the downstairs seating one had to pass through a throng of prostitutes, all of them eager to divert the willing guest from the spectacle at hand. By the time Josephine Baker performed there, the new owner, Paul Derval, had cleaned the dance hall out, claiming: "My work was to direct a theatre, not a bordello."

Josephine Baker's performances at the Folies-Bergère were just as phenomenal as her role in *La Revue Nègre*. In one scene she appeared completely nude except for a dress made of bananas, while in another scene she emerged from a giant Easter egg after it had descended from the ceiling. During the first dress rehearsal the egg opened prematurely, leaving Baker clinging tenuously to its side forty feet above the pit orchestra. She was lifted back up to safety, but not before two of the cast members fainted.

Set malfunctions were not the only worry for an up-and-coming performer. Tiffs between *vedettes* (female stars) were common during the heyday of the music hall. One of the most famous of these conflicts occurred between Josephine Baker and Mistinguett, a small-town girl who wowed French audiences before and after World War I with her seductive personality and legs so long and perfect they were insured for 500,000 francs. Although Mistinguett was already past her prime by the twenties—she was born in 1873—it was Josephine Baker's arrival on the scene that definitively usurped her. She retaliated by attacking Baker in the press, calling her "old banana tits" and "that vulgar woman."

Today the Folies-Bergère manages to maintain much of the allure that made it so popular during *les années folles* and it remains a draw for tourists. The entrance opens into an ostentatious mix of plush blue carpeting, brilliant gold curtains, and large ornate chandeliers, while the main hall features warm reddish hues, with intricate art nouveau designs etched into the gilded balconies. Onstage, dancers dressed in shimmering boas twirl in a furious blur of feathers while kicking can-cans worthy of Baker herself.

Josephine Baker, 1925. © Getty Images

lapín agíle

22 RUE LES SAULES · PHONE: 01.46.06.85.87 · MÉTRO: LAMARCK-CAULAINCOURT
WWW.AU-LAPIN-AGILE.COM · TUES–SUN: 9PM–2AM

GAZING DOWN FROM THE HEIGHTS OF THE RUE LES SAULES, THE LAPIN AGILE MAY SEEM FAR REMOVED FROM THE FRENETIC excitement of rue Pigalle, but during the twenties and thirties it was a popular jazz age destination that regularly featured jazz singers and musicians. It was here that, in the late teens, the jazz violin pioneer Stéphane Grappelli heard jazz for the first time. Several years later he would get his first gig here, playing popular ballads and music hall numbers on the cabaret's run-down piano.

Grappelli spent much of his childhood in and around the streets of Montmartre, living at 28 rue Montholon **C** up until his mother's death when he was four. When his father joined the military, Grappelli was left effectively parentless for the duration of World War I. He turned to busking as a means of supporting himself, and despite his hardships would reflect on those times with some fondness: "That was the best time for musicians, you know—no radio, no gramophone. If you want music,

Stéphane Grappelli and Django Reinhardt, 1938. © Getty Images

you must go to the musician!" It is easy to imagine the young Grappelli scurrying through the streets of Montmartre when they were still punctuated by windmills, vineyards, and rickety huts; when the top of La Butte was, in his words, "nothing, a desert." Sometimes he would retrieve materials from the local quarries for the artists of the Bâteau Lavoir (13 place Émile-Goudeau) ⓓ , whose residents included Picasso, Gris, and Modigliani. When his father returned from the war, the two moved into a small, cramped attic at 59b rue Rochechouart ⓔ , filled with cockroaches and mice. He acquired a harmonium and continued to develop his burgeoning musical talents. Throughout this period, Grappelli frequented the Lapin Agile to hear the poet Francis Carco recite his latest work, while the classical guitarist Alexandre Lagoya slept on the floor. A lifelong resident of Montmartre, Grappelli returned to the Lapin Agile often and considered it his favorite cabaret.

Upon entering the Lapin Agile today, one has the impression of being transported back a hundred years to La Butte's rustic, *Montmartois* past. With its upright piano, long white benches, shaded lamps, and numerous reproductions of Picasso's paintings (the originals that once hung here were sold to museums many years ago), the Lapin Agile provides a warm atmosphere in which to experience *chanson française* (traditional French music).

musée le placard d'erík satíe

6 RUE CORTOT · PHONE: 01.42.78.15.18 · MÉTRO: LAMARCK-CAULAINCOURT
BY APPOINTMENT ONLY

THE MUSÉE LE PLACARD D'ERIK SATIE DISPLAYS MEMORABILIA FROM THE LIFE OF ERIK SATIE, THE FAMED COMPOSER AND ASSOCIATE of Les Six who lived at 6 rue Cortot from 1890 to 1898. A lifelong eccentric, Satie started his own religion, "the Metropolitan Church of the Art of Jesus Conductor," in the 1890s, for which he wrote a manifesto railing against the excesses of contemporary classical music. Satie was one of the first composers to incorporate jazz influences into a serious orchestral work. In 1917 he co-wrote the ballet *Parade* with Jean Cocteau, which included a scene called the *Rag-Time du Paquebot*. Featuring odd sounds like a roulette wheel, a ship's siren, a typewriter, and several gunshots, the ballet so incensed the audience that a riot broke out as soon as the curtain dropped. Satie was later sued for libel and labeled a "cultural anarchist." Satie's vagaries were not limited to the musical sphere. He never talked while eating for fear of choking to death and only ate white foods such as eggs, sugar, and animal fat. Later on, he became known as the "velvet gentleman," for his extensive collection of velvet suits.

moulín de la galette

(NOW LE MOULIN DE LA GALETTE RESTAURANT AND CINÉMA DU MOULIN DE LA GALETTE)

LE MOULIN DE LA GALETTE RESTAURANT · 83 RUE LEPIC
PHONE: 01.46.06.84.77 · MÉTRO: ABBESSES · OPEN DAILY

CINÉMA DU MOULIN DE LA GALETTE · 1 AVENUE JUNOT
PHONE: 01.42.54.15.12 · MÉTRO: ABBESSES · WWW.CINE13.COM · OPEN DAILY

PAINTED BY RENOIR, PICASSO, TOULOUSE-LAUTREC, AND VAN GOGH, THE MOULIN DE LA GALETTE IS A MONTMARTRE LANDMARK AND the last of the thirty-odd windmills that used to grace the summit of La Butte. During the 1870s, its interior was converted into a *bal musette*, a hall catering to a largely working-class clientele eager to dance to the popular songs of the day. It would remain open for another ninety years, transforming itself first into a music hall, where customers would come to watch performances, and later, a movie theater. In the late 1930s, the Quintette du Hot Club de France made the Moulin de la Galette one of its principal venues.

Featuring violinist Stéphane Grappelli and guitarist Django Reinhardt, the Quintette is the most influential jazz group to have emerged from French soil. Much

Django Reinhardt, date unknown. © Roger-Viollet

44

of the Quintette's reputation can be traced to Reinhardt, a gifted, wildly eccentric gypsy who spent much of his life in caravans on the outskirts of Paris. Badly disfigured when his caravan burned down in 1928, Django lost the use of two fingers on his right hand and consequently developed an entirely new playing style to compensate for his deformity.

The Quintette was at its height while playing at the Moulin de la Galette. An outstanding recording remains of one of their nights at the venue, featuring the songs "Daphne," "Limehouse Blues," and "Swing Guitars," among others. Although perfectly in sync on stage, the Quintette was forever in danger of splitting up. Many of their difficulties can be attributed to Django's stubborn and fickle nature. As Grappelli once said: "In spring when leaves reappear, Django disappears." And this was by no means an overstatement, as the guitarist often missed concerts, recording sessions, and interviews due to inexplicable flights of fancy. On one occasion he decided to drive his car out to Toulon to see some relatives, but, a notoriously dangerous driver, he got into an accident while trying to pass another car on the highway. When the

Django's caravan, circa 1930s. Émile Savitry

police arrived on the scene they mistook the unkempt, licenseless gypsy for a thief and immediately hauled him to prison. Reinhardt tried to argue with them, claiming to be the most famous guitarist in Europe. It was to no avail. Left with little recourse, he took out his guitar and started to play a Neapolitan love song. Luckily for him, the police were immediately won over.

This wouldn't be the last time that Django's music would get him out of a bind. During World War II, Reinhardt was detained by the Nazis after a failed attempt to flee to Switzerland. Had the officer on duty not been a jazz fan, Django might have been executed for spying. Instead, he was released on the condition that he make no more efforts to escape.

Django Reinhardt occupied a hotel on the nearby place Émile Goudeau for several years during the thirties with his wife, children, and extended family. During this time he was treated like royalty, especially by his doting mother, Negros. Each day Negros would wake up early in the morning to iron Django's pants so they would be warm when he got dressed. Then she would leave the house with only five francs in her pocket and spend the day selling lace in order to scrape together enough money to pay for lunch. The rest of the family would only just be rising when she returned several hours later, her arms laden with bags of bread, wine, and cheese.

According to Django's close friend and biographer Charles Delaunay, the apartment looked like many other Montmartre garrets at the time. Its rooms were small, its wallpaper flowery and torn, and its curtains thin and drab, letting in "more dust than light." The most exceptional feature in the apartment was Reinhardt's monkey, which spent much of its time eating anything it could get its hands on, including refuse, soap, and sometimes even the rug.

Although the music hall of the Moulin de la Galette has long since closed down, the windmill still stands, housing both a restaurant and a small theater. During the summer, one often sees Parisians and tourists alike enjoying a French meal on the breezy, ivy-covered terrace, under the windmill's great fans.

former residence of
louis armstrong

(NOW HOTEL ALBA OPERA)

34 TOUR D'AUVERGNE · PHONE: 01.48.78.80.22
WWW.ALBA.HOTELSPARISOPERA.COM · MÉTRO: ST.-GEORGES

WHEN LOUIS ARMSTRONG CAME TO PARIS IN 1934 THERE WAS STILL A LARGE AND VIBRANT AFRICAN-AMERICAN community in Montmartre. Using this hotel as a base, Armstrong claimed he "lazied around Paris for three or four months (and) had lots of fun with musicians from the States—French cats too." Like many jazz musicians before him, Armstrong found that for the first time in his life he was considered an artist rather than simply a "colored entertainer."

No one could have idolized Armstrong's artistic ability more than Django Reinhardt, who broke down crying the first time he heard Armstrong on record. Django arranged a meeting as soon as he learned that the great trumpeter had settled in Montmartre. Unfortunately,

Louis Armstrong giving autographs during a concert in Paris, date unknown. © Roger-Viollet

49

their initial encounter proved to be a great disappointment. Django had hoped that Armstrong would sign him onto his band after hearing him play, but Armstrong was so busy getting dressed that he hardly even heard the guitarist. Apart from a cursory "Very good! Go on!" shouted from the dressing room, his performance went unacknowledged. Django left the session deflated, beads of sweat running down his face.

He was given a chance to redeem himself later that year when Bricktop called him over to her club at five in the morning to jam with Armstrong. Stéphane Grappelli, who was there at the time, said: "For the only time in my life I heard Louis sing, accompanied only by Django's guitar. There were no discussions to decide what key they'd play in or what tunes they'd choose. Louis began and Django followed him in the twinkling of an eye. It was a revelation for me, and all of us were entranced."

moulin rouge

82 BOULEVARD DE CLICHY · PHONE: 01.46.06.60.00 · MÉTRO: BLANCHE
WWW.MOULINROUGE.FR · OPEN DAILY: DINNER AT 7PM; SHOWS AT 9PM & 11PM

UNLIKE THE MOULIN DE LA GALETTE, THE MOULIN ROUGE WAS NEVER A FUNCTIONING WINDMILL. BUILT DURING FRANCE'S *BELLE époque* as a music hall, it thrived on Parisians' desire to celebrate after the disastrous Franco-Prussian War ended in 1871. And because it offered grand spectacles for a reasonable price, it soon became a favorite destination for worker and aristocrat alike. When it was built, the most remarkable feature of the Moulin Rouge was an enormous stucco elephant erected in the back garden. On any given day, a curious gentleman could climb into the beast's cavernous stomach, where a belly dancer was waiting to perform for a one-franc sum.

During the late twenties, the Moulin Rouge featured the jazz singer Adelaide Hall in a production of *Blackbirds*. Although now overlooked, Hall was a legendary performer during the interwar years. A collaborator of both Duke Ellington and Art Tatum, she helped launch Ellington's career with the hit song "Creole Love Call."

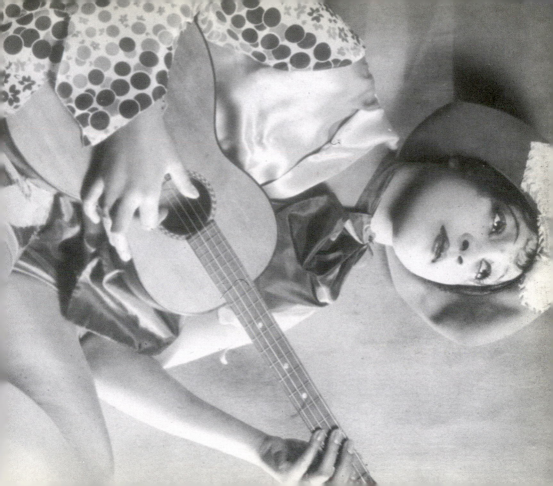

Hall's reputation was so great that when she first came to Paris, Josephine Baker announced a world tour rather than risk direct competition with the Broadway songstress. Before she left, however, Baker surreptitiously visited a performance to size up the competition. When she tried to slip out the back door of the Moulin Rouge, she was immediately mobbed by journalists looking for a juicy quote. Her boyfriend, Pepito, put his hand over her mouth and ushered her into the nearest cab.

The Parisian performance of *Blackbirds* was scandalous in comparison to its New York counterpart. An immense wooden facsimile of Adelaide Hall stood guard at the entrance, admitting guests through the space between its legs. During the show, Hall was dressed in revealing, flesh-colored outfits. As a result, Hall appeared fully nude to the audience when performing the "Diga Diga Do," her signature number about love in the jungle of Samoa.

Today one can dine on rich meals of foie gras, mussels, and beluga caviar while taking in the Moulin Rouge's spectacular nightly performances by a cast of sixty dancers. Featuring pillars plastered with old Toulouse-Lautrec posters, billowing red and white curtains, and opulent furnishings, the Moulin Rouge boasts a luxurious décor that successfully recreates the sumptuous atmosphere of Paris's *belle époque*. Reservations are highly recommended as this is a popular tourist destination.

site of the big apple

12

73 PLACE PIGALLE

OWNED AND MANAGED BY ADELAIDE HALL'S HUSBAND, BERT HICKS, THE BIG APPLE WAS INTENDED TO MIMIC A SLICE OF SOPHISTI- CATED Harlem in Paris. From 1937 to 1938 it accomplished just that, attracting famous guests ranging from the Duke and Duchess of Windsor to Cole Porter and Fats Waller. Each night, Hall would emerge from a cloud and descend a spiral stair-case to the stage below. She worked the audience in her unique style, mingling with the crowd and dancing on tables, effortlessly shifting from diva to flirt. Occasionally she would teach the audience a dance called the "Canned Apple." Described as a bewildering assortment of high kicks, gyrations, and splits, it was a curious mix of the Charleston, the Suzie-Q, truckin', the can-can, and the Praise Allah.

Adelaide Hall's reign as the queen of Montmartre ended prematurely when a famous duke became dangerously infatuated with her. He entered the club one night brandishing a knife and threatening to kill both himself and Hall. A guest at a neigh-boring table wrestled him to the ground, but Hall's fear remained and she soon took an engagement in London.

(A) new morning

7-9 RUE DES PETITES ÉCURIES · PHONE: 01.45.23.51.41 · MÉTRO: CHÂTEAU D'EAU
WWW.NEWMORNING.COM · MON–SAT: SHOWS START BETWEEN 9PM & 10PM

With room for more than four hundred guests, the New Morning is the largest and most famous jazz club in Paris today. Since opening its doors in 1981 the New Morning has consistently featured world-renowned jazz artists like Chick Corea, Jerry Gonzalez, and Ravi Coltrane. Ticket prices are usually between $7 and $12.

(B) le blue note

14 RUE MULLER · PHONE: 01.42.54.69.76 · MÉTRO: ANVERS OR BARBÈS
WED–SAT: SHOWS START BETWEEN 10PM & 11PM

Of no relation to the sixties club of the same name (see p.104), le Blue Note in Montmartre has been showcasing first-rate Brazilian jazz for the past twenty years, ranging in style from samba to bossa nova to blues. There is no cover charge, but there is a one-drink minimum.

houdon

5 RUE DES ABBESSES · PHONE: 01.46 06.35.91 · MÉTRO: PIGALLE OR ABBESSES
FRI & SAT: OPENS 10PM

A small jazz club located in an unassuming bistro on La Butte, the Houdon is a popular venue for up-and-coming musicians who have yet to establish themselves in Paris's competitive jazz scene. A good destination for those seeking inexpensive yet lively jam sessions. One-drink minimum.

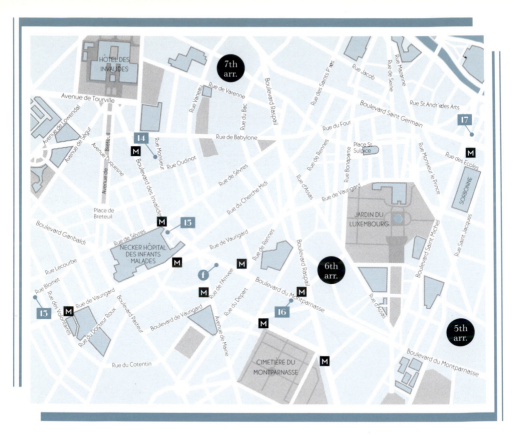

MONTPARNASSE

59

MONTPARNASSE

I F THE JAZZ AGE WAS BORN IN MONTMARTRE, IT GREW UP IN MONT-PARNASSE. BY THE 1930S, JAZZ MUSIC HAD REACHED THE QUARTER, trickling down from the heights of La Butte to cafés around the Carrefour Vavin and their expatriate customers like F. Scott Fitzgerald, Ernest Hemingway, and Henry Miller. In contrast to its Montmartre counterpart, however, Montparnasse's jazz scene was far less American in flavor. From the Caribbean fusion at the Bal Nègre to the gypsy stylings of Django Reinhardt, the clubs along the boulevard du Montparnasse played host to some of the world's first non-American jazz.

bal nègre
(NOW OPUS LATINO)

33 RUE BLOMET · PHONE: 01.40.61.08.66 · MÉTRO : SÈVRES-LECOURBE OR VOLONTAIRES
WWW.OPUSCLUB.FREE.FR/OPUS_LATINO.HTM · TUES–SAT: 8PM–2PM

THE BAL NÈGRE, WHICH WAS THE CENTER OF PARIS'S THRIVING CARIBBEAN COMMUNITY FOR MANY YEARS, WAS OPENED IN 1924 by Jean Rézard de Wouves to hold parties for his local political campaign. When it became apparent that the regulars preferred his piano playing to his speeches, de Wouves dedicated himself full-time to the club, naming it the Bal Coloniale and later the Bal Nègre.

At first the venue was geared exclusively towards the neighborhood's Caribbean population, featuring Martinique's national dance, the *beguine*. The atmosphere was similar to that of a Port-au-Prince ball: men and women lined up on opposite sides of the room while observers on the balcony took long sips of rum as they surveyed the scene. Women wore traditional Antillean clothes consisting of petticoats, handkerchiefs, and multicolored dresses stretching down to their heels.

The Bal Nègre soon began to attract members of Montparnasse's artistic community. The surrealists were the first to discover the establishment, drawn by the "primitiveness" of its regulars. Both André Masson and Joan Miró lived in the apartment next door. As the Bal Nègre welcomed these jazz age visitors, the venue's Caribbean musicians began to adapt their songs to the new sounds of America. As a result, a whole generation of Antillean jazz musicians emerged in the thirties including Felix Valvert, Robert Mavounzy, and Alexandre Stellio. Accomplished musicians in their own right, they collaborated with seminal figures like Django Reinhardt, Arthur Briggs, and Harold Cooper.

Today the Bal Nègre goes by the name of Opus Latino and features South American as well as Antillean music. Although the layout of the establishment has remained the same, with a large balcony encircling an often crowded dance floor, much of the décor has changed. The walls, painted in a warm palette of yellows, reds, and greens, now contain flags, photos, and a large picture of Che Guevara gazing out at the scene.

The Opus Latino also offers dance classes spanning a wide range of styles.

former residence of cole porter

13 RUE MONSIEUR

COLE PORTER LIVED AT THIS ADDRESS FROM 1920 TO 1937. GRAND-SON OF A MILLIONAIRE, PORTER SPENT HIS ENTIRE LIFE SUR-rounded by opulence, and his home at 13 rue Monsieur was no exception.

In the entryway, black-and-white checked tile led from the front door to a finely cut marble staircase flanked on each side by columns. From the top of the stairs, a grand salon stretched out over much of the first floor, enclosing in its white paneling soft velvet couches, oriental-finished tables, and colorful rugs. Platinum paper coated the library walls, while elsewhere in the house zebra-skin rugs complemented ornate art deco furnishing. According to Bricktop, Porter's workroom looked "like a monk's cell" amidst this lavish décor. The room, painted entirely in white, contained nothing but a white table, a white piano, and one hundred white pencils. The wall facing the courtyard was made of frosted glass with a small, clear porthole so that Porter could gaze outside for inspiration.

Perhaps the most spectacular room in the house was the ballroom, located in the basement. Featuring wood floors, mirrored walls, and a bandstand, the ballroom was the site of famous parties attended by Paris's leading socialites as well as Picasso, Noël Coward, and Jean Cocteau.

The building is now a private residence.

síte of la croíx du sud

3 BOULEVARD DU MONTPARNASSE

IN THE TWENTIES AND THIRTIES, THE BOULEVARD DU MONTPAR-
NASSE WAS LINED WITH JAZZ CLUBS, AND LA CROIX DU SUD WAS A
popular nightspot frequented by such luminaries as the film director Jacques Tati
and the painter Willem de Kooning. Home to Stéphane Grappelli's band in 1931, it
is also famous as the place where the violinist first met Django Reinhardt during a
show. According to André Ekyan, a saxophonist who was playing with Grappelli at
the time, Reinhardt had the "face of a Calabrian bandit" and stared at the band with
such intensity that Ekyan almost initiated a fight with him. Grappelli later recalled:
"I saw Django soon after I got back from Argentina…One night three or four persons
came into the club…They listened to us attentively and stared hard at us…in a way
that was, in reality, none too pleasant. They were of such dubious appearance that I
thought they might be gangsters, or worse still, gangsters who disliked our music…
I was almost sure I'd already seen the tallest of them [Django] playing the guitar in
the Paris streets. He came up to the band and made as though he wanted to have a
word with me. In the most extraordinary French he asked me to play a jazz number."

la coupole

102 BOULEVARD DU MONTPARNASSE
PHONE: 01.43.20.14.20 · MÉTRO: VAVIN
WWW.FLOBRASSERIES.COM/COUPOLEPARIS/
OPEN DAILY: 8AM–2AM

LA COUPOLE WAS ONE OF THE FIRST MONT-PARNASSE CLUBS TO BRING JAZZ TO THE Left Bank bohemian community. Much like the Bal Nègre, it employed musicians from the Caribbean who mixed elements of jazz with traditional Antillean songs like the *beguine*. For a brief period, La Coupole's jazz band even enjoyed some fame, cutting three records for the label Ultraphone.

Built in 1927 by two ex-employees of Le Dôme, La Coupole was a latecomer to the Montparnasse café scene. Nevertheless, it quickly attracted a large section of the intellectual expatriate crowd including Ernest

La Coupole, date unknown. © Roger-Viollet

Hemingway, Jean Cocteau, Giacometti, Man Ray, and his mistress Kiki. When La Coupole first opened, the owners commissioned thirty-two artists to paint the pillars propping up the main hall. It is still possible to see these works, painted by Fernand Léger, Marie Vassilieff, and Moise Kisling among others.

La Coupole continues to feature dancing, although today the music is likely to be electronic. On Tuesdays it is still possible to dance to salsa music late into the night.

petit cluny

32 RUE DE LA HARPE · MÉTRO : ST.–MICHEL

DURING WORLD WAR II THE STREETS OF MONTPARNASSE, SAINT-GERMAIN, AND THE CHAMPS-ÉLYSÉES WERE HOME TO AN ANTI-collaborationist youth movement called the *zazous*. Although very little of this jazz-inspired counterculture survives in Paris today, it is still possible to visit the Petit Cluny, a café that was once frequented by the *zazous*, or to dine at *Zazous* ❶ (48 boulevard du Montparnasse; 01.45.49.32.88; Métro: Falguière), a restaurant that aims to recreate the spirit of the age.

With a name based on the scat singing of Cab Calloway ("Zah-Zuh-Zah"), the movement drew heavily on American culture as a means to resist the Nazis. The members' choice of clothing, for example, was greatly influenced by California's zoot-suit fad. The men slicked their hair back and wore long, boxy, fur-lined jackets with many pockets. Their pants were short and cuffed, revealing colorful socks and shoes with enormous soles. Their shirts, which had abnormally high collars, were tightly secured by narrow ties. The women wore their nails long and their

skirts short and completed their outfits with high wooden platform shoes and long coats. Members of both sexes donned large black-framed glasses and carried "Neville Chamberlain" umbrellas. The *zazous* often threw surprise parties at cafés like the Petit Cluny, where they danced the jitterbug to big-band music.

In general, the *zazous* aimed to distance themselves from overt political statements, cultivating instead an aura of general disdain for Nazi collaborators. However, in 1942 the *zazous* started to wear yellow stars emblazoned with the word "swing" to show solidarity with Paris's Jewish population. Nazi retaliation against this affront was swift and brutal, with a few *zazous* sent to concentration camps. Matters only became worse after the Nazis finished deporting Paris's Jewish population. With little else left to target, French fascists focused their attention on the *zazous*. The collaborationist press wrote scathing articles about the movement, while La Jeunesse Populaire (the French equivalent of the Hitler Youth) began storming *zazous* dance-parties en masse and shaving the heads of any unfortunate males who happened to fall into their clutches.

Despite the attempts to crackdown on the *zazous* and their swing-inspired resistance, jazz's popularity and influence steadily increased during World War II. Much of the music's success can be attributed to Charles Delaunay, who worked tirelessly to protect jazz from Nazi censorship and devised a clever plan to save jazz from the Nazi ban on American products. Turning to New Orleans's French heritage, he claimed that jazz was in fact a French creation appropriated from old French shepherd songs and quadrilles. In order to complete the ruse he translated popular standards into French: "In the Mood" became "*Dans l'ambiance*," "Two Left Feet" became "*Deux pieds gauches*," and "Take the A-Train" became "*L'Attaque de train*." Delaunay also organized his own Resistance group out of the headquarters of the Hot Club de France, giving himself the code name "Benny" and calling the network "Cart," in honor of Benny Carter.

NOW PLAYING AROUND MONTPARNASSE

OPUS LATINO · 61

LA COUPOLE · 66

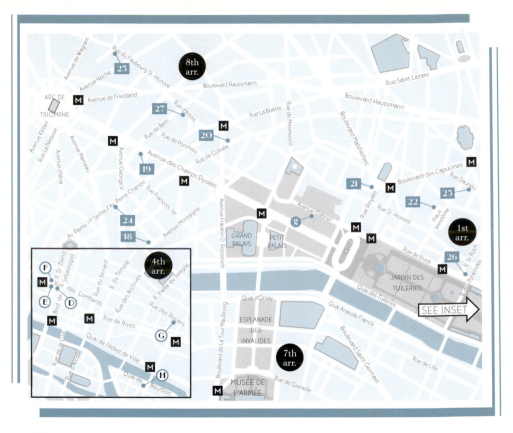

CHAMPS-ÉLYSÉES

18 THÉÂTRE DES CHAMPS-ÉLYSÉES

19 FORMER RESIDENCE OF JOSEPHINE BAKER

20 LE BOEUF SUR LE TOIT

21 MAXIM'S

22 HOTEL RITZ

23 HARRY'S NEW-YORK BAR

24 CALVADOS

25 SALLE PLEYEL

26 SLOW CLUB

27 SITE OF THE BLUE NOTE

8 CAFÉ DES AMBASSADEURS

(**D**) LE DUC DES LOMBARDS   (**E**) BAISER SALÉ

(**F**) SUNSET / SUNSIDE   (**G**) 7 LÉZARDS   (**H**) FRANC PINOT

M METRO STOP

75

CHAMPS-ÉLYSÉES

STRETCHING FROM THE ARC DE TRIOMPHE TO THE PLACE DE LA CONCORDE, THE AREA AROUND THE CHAMPS-ÉLYSÉES BOASTED A thriving population of expatriates during the jazz age, with many Americans preferring the quarter's bar-oriented nightlife to Montparnasse's café culture. The 8th *arrondissement* was also an important hub for the spread of jazz from the twenties to the fifties: Josephine Baker wowed French audiences with her first appearance in 1925 at the Théâtre des Champs-Élysées; thirty years later Dizzy Gillespie performed much the same feat at the Salle Pleyel, ushering in a new era of bebop with his legendary big band.

théâtre des champs-élysées

15 AVENUE MONTAIGNE · PHONE: 01.49.52.50.50 · MÉTRO: ALMA-MARCEAU
WWW.THEATRECHAMPSELYSEES.FR · CHECK WEBSITE FOR PERFORMANCE TIMES

BUILT IN 1913, THE THÉÂTRE DES CHAMPS-ÉLYSÉES DID NOT TAKE LONG TO BECOME A HAVEN FOR CONTROVERSIAL AND CUTTING-EDGE works. Shortly after opening, it featured Stravinsky's groundbreaking *The Rite of Spring*, which shocked the musical establishment with its dissonance. In 1925 the Théâtre des Champs-Élysées stunned Paris yet again when it presented Josephine Baker in *La Revue Nègre*.

Drawing on French fantasies of both Africa and African-Americans, the cast of *La Revue Nègre* included chorus men dressed in top hats and overalls, as well as a clarinet-toting Sidney Bechet playing the part of a poor fruit vendor. Most noteworthy, however, was *La Danse Sauvage*, a show-stopping finale in which an almost nude Josephine Baker wrapped herself around a half-naked male dancer.

The show was met with near-unanimous praise and word of its success soon spread throughout Paris's clubs and cafés. But while France may have been racially tolerant in comparison to segregationist America, critical responses to *La Revue Nègre* reveal underlying prejudices. For example, André Levinson of *L'Art Vivant* wrote that Josephine Baker had "the splendor of an ancient animal, until the movements of her behind and her grin of a benevolent cannibal make admiring spectators laugh." The critic Pierre de Regnier described Baker as a figure "who walks with bended knees...and looks like a boxing kangaroo...Is this a man? Is this a woman?"

Restored in 1987, the Théâtre des Champs-Élysées looks much the same as it did back in 1913. It is hard not to be impressed by the building's white marble façade with its finely etched scenes of dancers and musicians, or the large, colorful frescos gracing the inside of the lobby. However, these aspects pale in comparison to the splendor of the theater, whose ceiling consists of an enormous glass light cut in a floral pattern and encircled by pastoral scenes of ancient Greek muses and graces.

The Théâtre des Champs-Élysées presents music of all kinds including jazz, classical music, and world music.

former residence of josephine baker

77 CHAMPS-ÉLYSÉES

FROM HER EXPLOSIVE DEBUT IN *LA REVUE NÈGRE* IN 1925 UNTIL HER DEATH IN 1975, JOSEPHINE BAKER WAS A FRENCH NATIONAL icon. She appeared in numerous movies, released best-selling books, and performed onstage in front of sellout crowds. So great was her attachment to France that she joined the Resistance during World War II.

Baker lived in many different places during the twenties, but none was more impressive than her apartment at 77 Champs-Élysées. With interiors designed by the famous couturier Paul Poiret, the flat was nicknamed the "marble palace" for its numerous oriental tapestries, life-size statues of Josephine, and a huge marble swimming pool that dominated one of the rooms.

If Baker's onstage persona seemed sensational, it was tame in comparison to her real life. An avid collector of exotic animals, Baker owned enough pets for a small zoo, including a leopard named Chiquita that she often took on walks down the Champs-Élysées. Her menagerie of animals—which included monkeys, mice, parrots, dogs, cats, snakes, swans, goats, and pigs—moved with her from house to house over the course of several decades, increasing in size with each passing year.

Baker was also renowned for her amorous exploits. Some of her more famous lovers included Bricktop, Belgian mystery writer Georges Simenon, and Giuseppe Abatino, a Sicilian gigolo who masqueraded as an Italian count.

le boeuf sur le toît

34 RUE DU COLISÉE · PHONE: 01.43.59.83.80 · MÉTRO: SAINT-PHILIPPE DU ROULE
WWW.BOEUFSURLETOIT.COM · OPEN DAILY: NOON–1:30AM

NAMED AFTER A BALLET BY JEAN COCTEAU AND DARIUS MILHAUD, LE BOEUF SUR LE TOIT WAS ONE OF THE MOST POPULAR ESTAB-lishments for Parisian intellectuals from 1922 until World War II. Although it's now situated at 34 rue du Colisée, Le Boeuf sur le Toit started out as the Gaya in the rue Duphot and then moved to the rue Boissy d'Anglas, before settling in its present loca-tion in 1941. Translated literally as "The Ox on the Roof," Le Boeuf sur le Toit was frequented by Dadaists like Tristan Tzara and Francis Picabia. Its most famous regu-lar, however, was Jean Cocteau, who held court at the restaurant in the twenties.

Cocteau played an important role in introducing Paris's artistic elite to jazz dur-ing the teens and twenties. He witnessed firsthand the birth of jazz in the city, writing about Louis Mitchell at the Casino de Paris as early as 1918. He also performed some of the first spoken word poetry, releasing a recording of his poems with an accompa-nying jazz band. At Le Boeuf sur le Toit he played drums with the house band.

Often in the audience were Cocteau's friends and collaborators, Les Six, which included Arthur Honegger, Louis Durey, Germaine Tailleferre, Darius Milhaud, Georges Auric, and Francis Poulenc. Les Six was a collection of classical composers closely tied to Cocteau and his aesthetic theories. Over the course of the twenties they would integrate the music they heard at Le Boeuf sur le Toit into their compositions, producing several classical pieces with a jazz bent. Les Six were soon joined by many other luminaries including Maurice Ravel, Pablo Picasso, Max Jacob, Fernand Léger, Erik Satie, and Marcel Duchamp. The writer Maurice Sachs described Le Boeuf sur le Toit as a place where "Society mingled with painters and actors, men of affairs with writers. It was not unusual to meet these working men in sandals come down from Montparnasse. Parisians as well as tourists had only to consult a

82 *Benny Carter, 1936. Benny Carter Collection, Archives Center, National Museum of American History, Behring Center, Smithsonian Institution*

reputable Paris guidebook to encounter le Boeuf and its wonders. As one tourist guide described, there one could find 'the artistic trend of the moment, the literary trend of the moment, and...*the* trend of the moment, whatever it may be.'"

When Le Boeuf sur le Toit first opened, its resident pianist was the classical composer Jean Wiener. A virtuosic performer, Wiener was known to astound his audience by reading a detective novel while playing a popular jazz number, flipping the pages of the book without missing a single beat. As the popularity of jazz increased in France, Le Boeuf sur le Toit became a rallying point for local and visiting musicians like Django Reinhardt and Benny Carter. Long improvisational sessions became so commonplace at Le Boeuf sur le Toit that the French expression for jam session is now *faire le boeuf.*

Benny Carter played frequently at Le Boeuf sur le Toit during his three-year stay in Europe. A dynamic performer, he remained at the forefront of the jazz scene from the twenties well into the late nineties, working as an alto saxophonist, arranger, bandleader, and composer. When he first arrived on French soil, he was a wanted man in the United States, having illegally taken his daughter with him following the loss of a custody battle. Upon arriving in Cherbourg, however, Carter was notified by the French police that he was wanted for kidnapping and would likely be imprisoned if he went back to America. He decided to return his daughter to her mother, and a month later, after the charges were dropped, he finally made it to Paris.

Although Le Boeuf sur le Toit no longer features nightly jazz, it has managed to preserve much of its charm. A vaulted expanse of skylights, ferns, and classic twenties décor, the restaurant spans multiple levels, and proudly displays a reproduction of Francis Picabia's *L'Oeil Cacody* in the entrance. The original was transferred to a museum after hanging in the establishment for many years.

maxím's

3 RUE ROYALE · PHONE: 01.42.65.27.94 · MÉTRO: CONCORDE
WWW.MAXIMS-DE-PARIS.COM · MON–SAT:12:30PM–2PM; 7:30PM–10PM

OPENED IN 1893 BY MAXIM GAILLARD AS A RESTAURANT FOR COACH-MEN, MAXIM'S QUICKLY TRANSFORMED INTO THE MOST POPULAR destination for Paris's *jeunesse dorée* (golden youth). In 1899, the restaurant was remodeled into its present art nouveau décor, where beveled mirrors, gilded leaves, and copper ornaments compete with the food for the attention of diners. At the turn of the last century, Maxim's catered mostly to aristocrats, but following World War I, its appeal broadened, attracting guests like Charlie Chaplin and Jean Cocteau, and becoming a vibrant center of the jazz age.

After the arrival of jazz with *La Revue Nègre*, Maxim's was one of the first sophisticated establishments to open its doors to a phenomenon sweeping through Paris, *les dancings*, inspired by African-American dance steps that traveled through the city in progressive waves over the course of the twentieth century. One of the first such dances, the cakewalk, arrived in France around 1900, filtering through salons before making its way to Paris's numerous music halls. Originally designed by slaves to mock their owners' dainty manners, it became an instant hit among upper-class Parisians tired of older steps like the waltz. The cakewalk was an improvisational dance traditionally performed in a competitive setting, where rival dancers would vie for a cake (hence the name "cakewalk" and terms like "that takes the cake"). The cakewalk was soon followed by other steps with names like "the grizzly bear," the "black bottom," and the "shimmy," before culminating in the Charleston. The Charleston had originated in a small African-American community located on an island off the coast of Charleston, South Carolina, and became wildly popular during the twenties. With roots in West African music, the Charleston is danced to a syncopated rhythm, and consists in kicking the heels outward while swinging the arms back and forth from the elbow.

Impressed by Josephine Baker's spectacular mastery of the Charleston, many lunchtime patrons decided they would rather dance than dine, prompting many of Paris's premier restaurants to hire their own jazz bands. Headed by French big-band star Fred Adison, Maxim's house band was lead by French big-band star Fred Adison and included Joseph Ginsburg, father of the controversial singer/songwriter Serge

Gainsbourg.

Today Maxim's continues to serve refined French cuisine, matched only by the dazzling allure of its décor. Sweeping pastoral scenes grace the walls, while in one room, an intricate stained-glass design of branches on a lemon tree decorates the ceiling. Maxim's still presents *dancings* on Friday nights, only now they're presided over by a DJ—not a jazz band—and the music is far more modern in flavor.

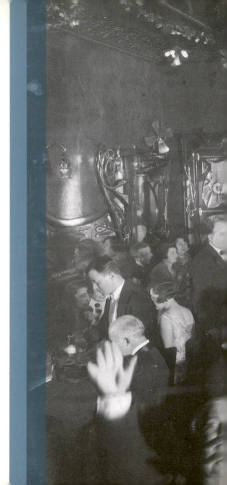

· *Maxim's, 1925. © Roger-Viollet*

89

hotel rítz

15 PLACE VENDÔME · PHONE: 01.43.16.33.65 · MÉTRO: OPÉRA
WWW.RITZ.COM · HEMINGWAY BAR OPEN MON–SAT: 6:30PM–2AM

DURING THE JAZZ AGE, THE HOTEL RITZ, LONG A GLAMOROUS MEET-ING PLACE FOR PARIS'S ARISTOCRATS, INTERNATIONAL FINANCIERS, and celebrities, was a favorite destination for American expatriates such as Ernest Hemingway, Cole Porter, and F. Scott Fitzgerald. When the Ritz first opened its doors, its two bars were segregated by gender with the women's bar (now the Hemingway bar) on the right and the men's bar on the left. During the twenties, it was not uncommon to see Cole Porter spending a lazy afternoon in the largely homosexual left bar. In 1919 he wrote a short song about his experiences there:

I simply adorn a secluded corner,
A cozy corner in the Ritz Hotel.
When I wander each afternoon for tea,
'Cause I like to see the kings

And let the queens see me
In my corner, my dear little corner
Where I gather up the spicy bits.

Porter would go on to produce many more songs in the ensuing decade, becoming one of America's premier songwriters. In 1928, he staged one of his first reviews at the Café des Ambassadeurs (1-3 avenue Gabriel) 🕄 featuring Frankie Gershwin and Sidney Bechet. On the opening night George Gershwin joined the ensemble, accompanying his sister on piano while she belted out a medley of his most popular songs. Although he was not a jazz musician, Porter had an enormous effect upon the shape of jazz. With harmonic structures that lend readily to improvisation, songs like "Night and Day," "Love for Sale," and "I've Got You under My Skin" quickly became jazz standards.

During the twenties, a Parisian socialite wrote about seeing Porter and Fitzgerald at the Ritz Bar: "He (Porter) introduced me to the Duke of Alba who was costumed as a chorus man and trailing a dog named Snookums on a silver chain. An odd subject. Hurried from this exalted society around the corner and saw remains of Scott Fitzgerald propped on a chair. Fled before recognition could ensue."

harry's new-york bar

5 RUE DAUNOU · PHONE: 01.42.61.71.14 · MÉTRO: OPÉRA
WWW.HARRYS-BAR.FR · OPEN DAILY: NOON–3AM

IKE THE RITZ HOTEL, HARRY'S NEW-YORK BAR WAS A POPULAR RETREAT FOR JAZZ AGE EXPATRIATES. ITS MOST FAMOUS MUSICAL guest was George Gershwin, who is rumored to have composed part of *An American in Paris* on the piano downstairs during his stay in Paris in the spring of 1928.

While composing *An American in Paris* Gershwin stayed at 19 avenue Kléber. Visitors to his room recalled being met by a cigar-smoking Gershwin, sitting in front of his impressive Pleyel piano. In one corner of the room lay a modest table with a deck of cards splayed out on top. Ira and George Gershwin spent many hours playing poker, while their sister, Frankie, gallivanted around town. In another corner of the room there was an odd collection of taxi horns that Gershwin had picked up on a trip down the avenue de la Grande Armée. They would later be incorporated into the score of *An American in Paris* to evoke the feel of Parisian traffic.

Long after Gershwin's departure, the piano downstairs at Harry's New-York Bar

Harry's New-York Bar, circa 1930s. Private Collection

ADRESSE :

est renseigné et envoyé par

HARRY'S NEW-YORK BAR

(Just Tell The Taxi Driver Sank Roo Doe Noo)
Tele: OPERA 73-00

5 , R u e D a u n o u - P A R I S

qui serait très heureux que vous donniez toute satisfaction à son Client.

Il espère que vous lui rendrez sa politesse à la première occasion.

HARRY Mc ELHONE, propriétaire.

was used by the ragtime pianist Glover Compton, who regularly entertained tourists with his syncopated stylings during the thirties. Apart from a few new wall hangings, Harry's New-York Bar has remained virtually unchanged since 1911, providing a slice of old Irish New York in the center of Paris. Much like it was in the 1920s and 1930s, American college flags, English public school memorabilia, scarves, shields, photos, and beer steins continue to crowd its wooden paneled walls. Harry's New-York Bar also claims to be the birthplace of several famous drinks, including the Bloody Mary, the Sidecar, and the White Lady.

calvados

40 AVENUE PIERRE LE PREMIER DE SERBIE · PHONE: 01.47.20.31.39. · MÉTRO: GEORGE V
OPEN DAILY: 10PM–6AM

"LITTLE" JOE TURNER PLAYED IN THIS QUAINT PIANO BAR FOR NEARLY THIRTY YEARS STARTING IN THE 1960S. A FORMER ACCOMPANIST to Adelaide Hall, he came to Paris with her during the thirties and immediately fell in love with the city and the French way of life. The start of World War II forced him to leave in 1939, and he would not return for another twenty years. "Little" Joe Turner played stride piano in the tradition of James P. Johnson and Fats Waller, with his left hand playing melody while the right hand provided rhythm and harmonies.

salle pleyel

252 RUE DU FAUBOURG-ST.-HONORÉ · PHONE: 01.45.61.53.00 · MÉTRO: TERNES
PERFORMANCES VARY

ERECTED IN 1927 BY THE PIANO MANUFACTURER CAMILLE PLEYEL, THE SALLE PLEYEL HAS FEATURED AN ASTONISHING RANGE OF JAZZ musicians over the years, from Louis Armstrong to Lester Young, Gerry Mulligan to Thelonious Monk.

Its most famous jazz concert occurred in 1948, when Dizzy Gillespie's big band bowled over the French public, lulled by the swing music of the war years, with the explosive sounds of bebop. According to promoter Charles Delaunay, "The general astonishment was such that, after the first number, the public completely forgot to applaud, as if stunned by the violence and stridency of the orchestra."

It's a wonder the band managed to pull off such a successful show. The musicians were exhausted and underfed, having just arrived in Paris from a tumultuous, unpaid Scandinavian tour. Moreover, their sheet music had disappeared on the day of the performance and they were forced to play by memory. In his biography, the drummer Kenny Clarke recalls the experience:

> *If I hadn't seen it with my own eyes, I wouldn't have believed it. The band, to a man, played all of the parts correctly for the entire program. And, mind you, it had been together for less than a year.*
>
> *I remember saying to Benny Bailey, when I heard about the missing music, "What the hell are we gonna do now?" And Benny said, "No trouble—we just hit! We've been playing that same music for a month already now. We know it ass backwards." And that's what made it great. We played without musical stands. Everybody stood up and the people just couldn't understand how we could play like that without music.*
>
> *It was a marvelous idea—and, of course, it was Dizzy's way of doing things, which I think is fantastic. It was the most fantastic thing that I've ever witnessed. You know, playing the same music every night. I've never done that, and the more we played it, the better it got.*

In the liner notes to the Vogue release of the Pleyel recordings, the author notes:

"The attack is of such unforgettable brutality that it can only be described as a punch in the face." The concert permanently fractured France's jazz community, pitting traditional fans of New Orleans and swing jazz against a younger generation of beboppers.

Another famous guest at the Salle Pleyel was Coleman Hawkins. One of the first great jazz saxophonists, Hawkins's harmonically complex improvisational style anticipated many later innovations in bebop. He visited Paris frequently during the thirties and forties, often collaborating with Django Reinhardt, Stéphane Grappelli, and Benny Carter. During his first trip to Paris, Hawkins played at the Salle Pleyel, and was so nervous that he made Hugh Panassié fill the first three rows with women to make him feel more at ease. In subsequent visits, Hawkins became more comfortable and began playing in the smaller clubs of Montmartre and Saint-Germain. On one such occasion a French jazz enthusiast recalled: "he

Jonah Jones playing at Paris Jazz Festival All-Stars, Salle Pleyel, 1946.
© Getty Images

99

played in a little joint on the rue Pigalle, somewhere like that, and everybody was crying, even the man at the door was crying, Hawk could play so much, with such feeling."

The Salle Pleyel presents both jazz and classical music and is home to the Orchestre de Paris (01.45.61.65.60, www.orchestredeparis.com) from October to Easter as well as several other orchestras.

Coleman Hawkins, 1948. © Roger-Viollet

slow club

130 RUE DE RIVOLI · PHONE: 01.42.33.84.30 · MÉTRO: CHÂTELET
TUES–SAT: SHOWS USUALLY START BETWEEN 10PM & 11PM

DATING BACK A HALF-CENTURY AND BURIED TWO STORIES UNDER-GROUND, THE SLOW CLUB IS ONE OF THE LAST OF THE JAZZ *CAVES* (cellars) remaining from the post–World War II era. In its heyday, the Slow Club featured regular performances by French jazz greats like Stéphane Grappelli and Django Reinhardt.

It is still possible to hear swing music played by musicians of Claude Luter's caliber. Bandleader for Sidney Bechet throughout the fifties, Luter has been at the center of Parisian jazz for more than fifty years. Long before his collaborations with Bechet, Luter directed one of the most popular big bands of the forties, the Lorientais. Although Luter respected and admired Bechet, not all of his memories are fond:

[Bechet] loved to find girls, but, if anyone in the band found a girl that Sid-

ney liked the look of, he would show his displeasure by cutting out all that musician's solos, often for nights on end, sometimes whole weeks...He did this to me—stopped my solos—but I made it clear to him that I wasn't going to have that sort of interference in my private life.

At the turn of the last century, the space now occupied by the Slow Club was used to store bananas en route to Les Halles market. The subterranean venue continues to attract regulars with its vintage, fifties-era décor. On a busy night, the Slow Club quickly heats up as dancers crowd the floor, while music fans and loyal regulars watch from red upholstered benches lining the club's dark brick walls. Music alternates between swing and fifties rock depending on the night.

site of the blue note

27 RUE D'ARTOIS

TWENTY-SEVEN RUE D'ARTOIS WAS ONCE THE HOME OF THE BLUE NOTE, A FAMOUS JAZZ CLUB IMMORTALIZED IN BERTRAND TAVER- nier's film about Lester Young and Bud Powell called '*Round Midnight*. The movie is based on the real-life experiences of Francis Paudras, a dedicated jazz fan who took in the mentally unstable Bud Powell during the late fifties and cared for him. The Blue Note was a long, narrow club with a bar on the right and a dance floor and stage in the back.

Powell was forbidden to drink alcohol due to his severe mental problems, but he often tried to convince unsuspecting guests to buy him a drink. Most of the time the bartender fooled him by rubbing the cork from a bottle of rum around the top of a glass of coke in order to simulate the taste of alcohol.

Like Powell, Young also spent his final days at the Blue Note, entertaining a crowd that on some nights was smaller than the band itself. The guitarist Jimmy Gourley later recalled some of Lester's antics while on stage:

Bud Powell, early 1960s. Francis Paudras

You should have seen him call the bartender while we were in the middle of a song. He'd blow a deep note, foghorn-style, then he'd make this elaborate ceremonial gesture, cracking everyone up in the process; and the bartender, who had immediately understood, would bring him his drink. He had a code: "a soft one" was wine; "a hard one" was vodka and Pernod.

Young's performances at the Blue Note marked his last public appearances. On March 15, 1959, a day after returning from Paris to New York, he died of complications due to alcoholism.

le duc des lombards

42 RUE DES LOMBARDS · PHONE: 01.42.33.22.88 · MÉTRO: CHÂTELET
MONDAY–SATURDAY: 8PM–1AM

Situated on the rue des Lombards, the new center of Paris's jazz scene, Le Duc des Lombards is a premier jazz club featuring famous French musicians such as Martial Solal, Henri Texier, and Aldo Romano. Although concerts typically start at 9:30pm, guests are welcome to come earlier for a meal in the restaurant upstairs.

baiser salé

58 RUE DES LOMBARDS · PHONE: 01.42.33.37.71 · MÉTRO: CHÂTELET
OPEN DAILY: 8PM–6AM

Featuring salsa, African, and Latin jazz, the Baiser Salé has a convivial atmosphere, where interaction with the band is encouraged.

sunset / sunside

60 RUE DES LOMBARDS · PHONE: 01.40.26.46.60 · MÉTRO: CHÂTELET
WWW.SUNSET-SUNSIDE.COM
OPEN DAILY: SUNSIDE CONCERTS START AT 9PM; SUNSET CONCERTS START AT 10PM

Sunset and Sunside are two first-class jazz clubs housed within the same building. Located on the ground floor, the Sunside focuses on acoustic jazz, showcasing musicians ranging from Aldo Romano to Ravi Coltrane. In the basement, the Sunset pumps out funkier and more electronic music, featuring fusion drawing on world beat, turntablism, and Latin jazz.

7 lézards

10 RUE DES ROSIERS · PHONE: 01.48.87.08.97 · MÉTRO: ST.-PAUL
WWW.7LEZARDS.COM · OPEN DAILY: SHOWS USUALLY START AT 10PM

Located in the heart of the Marais, the 7 Lézards features local musicians in a laid-back atmosphere. The ground floor bar/restaurant serves food and drink all day, while a basement club presents music at night.

franc pinot

I QUAI BOURBON · PHONE: 01.46.33.60.64 · MÉTRO: CHÂTELET
TUE–SAT: SHOWS START BETWEEN 9:30PM & 10PM

This relatively new addition to the 1st *arrondissement*'s thriving community of jazz clubs mixes live performances with traditional French cuisine. The Franc Pinot specializes primarily in vocal jazz and bebop, but branches out to other genres on weekends.

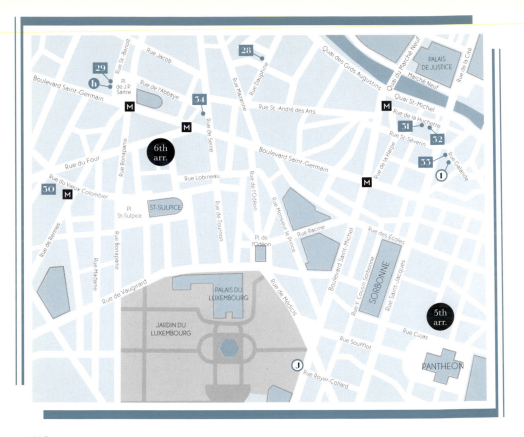

SAINT-GERMAIN-DES-PRÉS

SAINT-GERMAIN-DES-PRÉS

SHORTLY AFTER WORLD WAR II, FRANCE'S EXISTENTIALIST MOVE-
MENT, LED BY JEAN-PAUL SARTRE AND SIMONE DE BEAUVOIR, SET
up camp in the narrow streets of Saint-Germain-des-Prés. Although some "existentialists" were familiar with Sartre's brand of philosophy, most simply adopted the
trappings of the movement, wearing American-style clothes, reading detective nov-
els, and spending long hours in the quarter's numerous jazz clubs. Located in Saint-
Germain's medieval cellars, these clubs became known as *caves* and their regulars
troglodytes. In contrast to previous decades, jazz in the forties and fifties developed
into a harmonically and melodically more complex form of music called bebop, and
featured such premier American musicians as Bud Powell and Miles Davis. Because
its melodies were often intricate and difficult for dancing, bebop was initially considered too complicated and cerebral for the mainstream public. However, bebop now
enjoys wide popularity, and is often credited with having shifted jazz away from the
realm of popular music towards fine art.

tabou

(NOW CAFÉ LAURENT)

33 RUE DAUPHINE · PHONE: 01.43. 29.43.43 · MÉTRO: ODÉON
OPEN DAILY: 6:30PM–12:30AM; PERFORMANCES THUR–SAT

FOR A BRIEF PERIOD TABOU WAS THE CENTER OF SAINT-GERMAIN'S EXISTENTIALIST YOUTH MOVEMENT, WHICH MARRIED JAZZ CULTURE with the intellectual life of the Latin Quarter. The existentialist community was drawn to jazz, and in particular the new sub-genre of bebop, with its complex, lightning-fast sounds. Much like the *zazous* before them, these "existentialists" had their own dress code. The men wore multicolored cowboy shirts and canvas running shoes, while the women dressed in black shirts and pants. At its height, the Tabou was so popular that a membership card was required to gain entrance. Some of its more famous guests included Raymond Queneau, Jean-Paul Sartre, and Albert Camus.

The French author, critic, and trumpeter Boris Vian held court at the Tabou during the late forties, playing in the house jazz band and even writing a "tourist guide" of Saint-Germain-des-Prés. In it he describes the Tabou as "a long vaulted passage, like a subway station only much smaller and dirtier, bordered on one side by a stage decked out like a straw hut and on the other by an oak bar and a little nook designated as the cloak room. It took some time to make all this out, since the cigarette smoke produced a fog of London-like proportions."

Much like Jean Cocteau, Vian helped bridge the gap between jazz and Paris's intellectual elite. He socialized with his former teacher, Jean-Paul Sartre, and Sartre's partner, Simone de Beauvoir, and introduced them both to Saint-Germain-des-Prés' subterranean nightlife. When he was not playing traditional jazz, Boris Vian wrote several books, including the cult classic *I Shall Spit on Your Grave*. A story of race relations in America's Deep South, the book "borrowed" heavily from works by Richard Wright and Chester Himes. Its graphic depiction of violence, racism, and sexuality won it immediate popularity among France's youth, transforming Vian into a national symbol of revolt against the establishment. Vian's premature death in 1959

Le Tabou, 1947. Robert Doisneau © Agence Rapho, Photo by: Adam Rzepka. CNAC / MNAM / Dist. Réunion des Musées Nationaux / Art Resource, NY

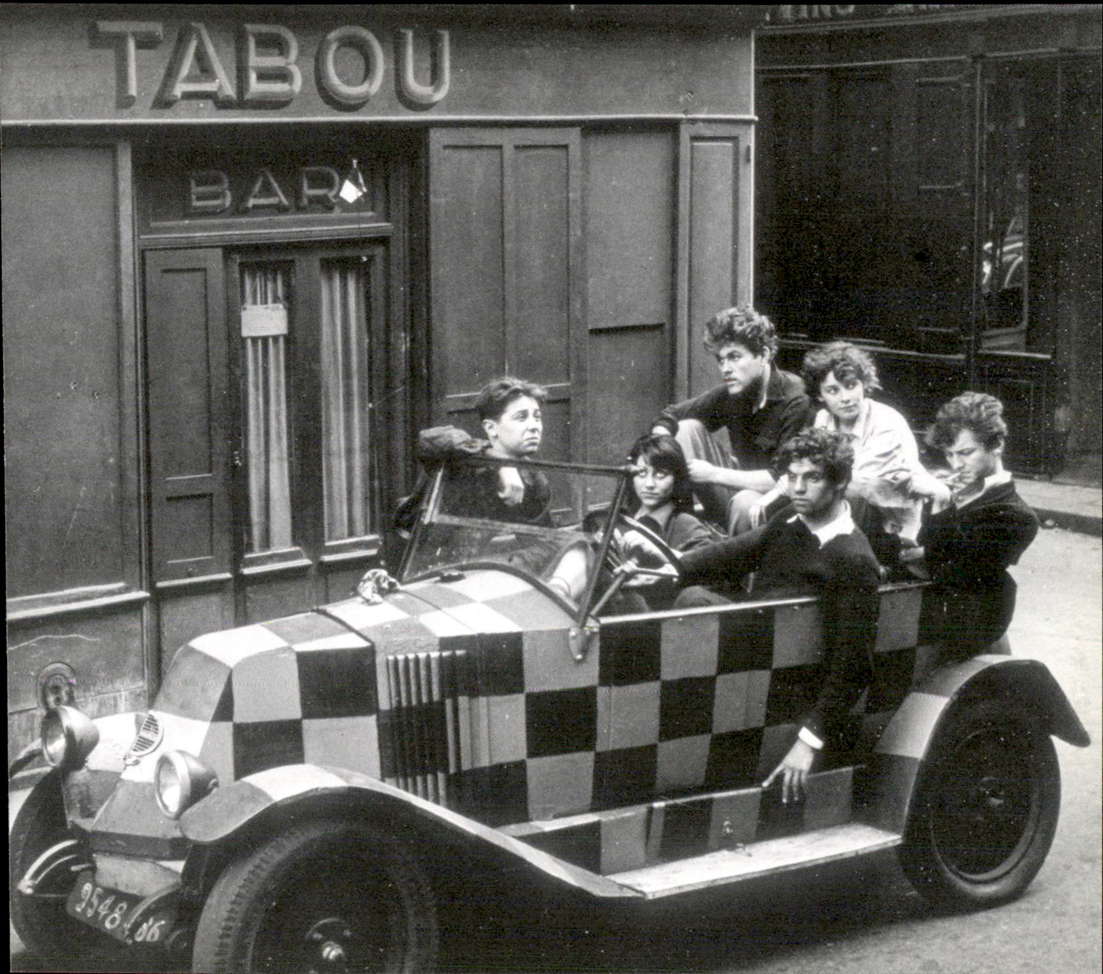
TABOU
BAR

at the age of thirty-nine sealed his reputation as the quintessential rebel—the French equivalent of James Dean.

After a year at the Tabou, Vian went on to found the Club Saint-Germain-des-Prés. The Tabou has changed hands many times since the forties and at this location there is now a piano bar called the Café Laurent.

club saint-germain-des-prés

FOUNDED BY BORIS VIAN AND FRÉDÉRIC CHAUVELOT FOLLOWING A DISAGREEMENT WITH THE OWNERS OF TABOU, THE CLUB SAINT-Germain-des-Prés soon became the new hub of the quarter's nightlife. In contrast to its current smart décor, the Club Saint-Germain-des-Prés of the forties was a gritty *cave*, stretching over three vaulted basement rooms. The walls were adorned with a wide variety of outlandish objects including a cardboard cutout of a horse's head, a picture of a bearded woman, and several large wooden sculptures salvaged from an old merry-go-round, which itself had been built from the wreckage of a sixteenth-century frigate.

Although a majority of the Tabou clientele followed Vian to the new locale, the atmosphere proved to be markedly different. Paris's "existentialist" youth culture had been discovered by mainstream French society, resulting in higher prices and larger crowds. In order to maintain the youthful spirit of the club, the organizers began hosting special events like *Nuit 1925* (Night of 1925) where guests dressed like flappers from the twenties, and *Nuit de l'Innocence* (Night of Innocence) where visitors dressed in white to protest accusations from other *caves* that the Club Saint-Germain-des-Prés encouraged immorality.

This initial exuberance soon gave way to a more professional atmosphere, where the jazz musicians were the main attraction. Duke Ellington headlined the opening night of the Club Saint-Germain-des-Prés, and it went on to present some of the biggest names in jazz, including Charlie Parker, Bud Powell, Max Roach, and Coleman Hawkins. Throughout the forties and fifties, the Club Saint-Germain-des-Prés was the center for bebop in Paris.

Many jazz musicians have vivid memories of their experiences at the club. Miles Davis, for example, recounts being deeply saddened after seeing a diminished Bud Powell perform at the Club Saint-Germain-des-Prés:

Man, everyone was just embarrassed as hell to see him like that, too embarrassed even to say a word, so we just had weak smiles on our faces...There was complete silence...Then I just jumped up and went and hugged Bud and told

Miles Davis, 1955. © Getty Images

him, "Bud, now you know you shouldn't be playing when you've been drinking like you have; now you know that, don't you?" I looked at him straight in the eyes and I said this loud enough for everyone to hear...Buttercup [Powell's wife] just stood, almost crying, grateful for what I had done...That was a sad sight, man, seeing and hearing Bud like that. I'll never forget it as long as I live.

Miles Davis visited Paris frequently over the course of his life, often playing at the Club-Saint-Germain-des-Prés. During his first trip to Paris he met and fell in love with the French singer and actress Juliette Greco. Though neither could speak the other's language, in his memoirs Davis recalled that Greco was "the first woman that I loved as an equal human being." Greco introduced Davis to Jean-Paul Sartre, and the pair immediately hit it off,

Club Saint-Germain, 1949. Willy Ronis © Mission du Patrinoine Photographique. Photo: Adam Rzepka. CNAC / MNAM / Dist. RMN / Art Resource, NY

pursuing discussions on jazz and philosophy late into the night. Davis would later claim that because of these conversations he deserved some credit for the creation of existentialism.

During the last few years of his life, Django Reinhardt also played at the Club Saint-Germain-des-Prés, conveniently located across the street from his home at the Hotel Crystal (24 rue St.-Benoît) **h** . At first Django felt out of place among so many young musicians, but he soon adjusted:

> *Oh yes they give me a bad time now and again, these little kids who think it's all happening, that we're no good anymore, that we're finished! But one day I got angry; I began to play so fast they couldn't follow me! And I gave them some new numbers to play, with difficult sequences. And there again they were all at sea! They've got some respect for me now!*

Although the cellar of the Club Saint-Germain-des-Prés has since been transformed into an after-hours nightclub, it is still possible to hear jazz in the plush upstairs bar/restaurant.

Charlie Parker (center) at Club Saint-Germain-des-Prés, 1949. Private Collection

théâtre du vieux-colombier

21 RUE DU VIEUX-COLOMBIER · PHONE: 01.44.39.87.00 · MÉTRO: SAINT-SULPICE
WWW.COMEDIE-FRANCAISE.FR · PERFORMANCES: TUES AT 7PM; WED–SAT AT 8PM; SUN AT 4PM

OPENED IN 1913, THE THÉÂTRE DU VIEUX-COLOMBIER HAS PRE-SENTED A WIDE RANGE OF AVANT-GARDE PLAYS AND LIVE MUSIC over the years. In 1917 Francis Poulenc, a classical composer and member of Les Six, staged one of the first jazz influenced classical pieces here called *Rhapsodie Nègre*. Soon after Tabou introduced jazz to Saint-Germain, the Théâtre du Vieux-Colombier followed suit, opening a *cave* in its cellar. During the fifties, the Vieux-Colombier was the primary center for traditional jazz in Paris and served as the home base for Sidney Bechet.

Bechet first came to Paris after a tumultuous tour in England, which had reputedly begun with his kidnapping from the steps of the Shelburn Hotel in Brighton Beach, Brooklyn, by the early bandleader, Will Marion Cook. His second trip to Paris in 1949, following a near-twenty-year absence, occurred under much more fortuitous circumstances. In fact, Bechet was so delighted by the warm welcome and ample work opportunities that he decided to settle there permanently. According to those who worked under him, Bechet was a fiery bandleader who often enjoyed putting his musicians in awkward situations. He shocked the trombonist Bob Mielke one night by announcing unexpectedly, "*Body and Soul* featuring Bob Mielke." Unfamiliar with the tune, the terrified Mielke had to fake his way through the song. However, for all Bechet's bravado and bluster, he experienced terrible stage fright before every performance.

Over the course of the next decade, Bechet's popularity steadily increased, and by the mid-fifties riots were breaking out in the ticket lines for his concerts. In one especially violent incident, hundreds of ticketless fans lifted up the box office outside the concert hall and carried it away while the ticket seller was still inside. Despite his great popularity, Bechet was forever afraid of competition from other jazz musicians. The saxophonist Benny Waters related a telling incident that occurred after Waters moved to France in 1953. During a guest appearance at the Vieux-Colombier, Waters made the grave mistake of playing the soprano saxophone, Bechet's signature instrument. A few days later Bechet cornered Waters in a dressing room, took out his revolver, started to polish it, and then said, "I never know when I might have to use this, you know." Benny Waters took the hint. It was a long time before he would play the soprano saxophone again.

Bechet's popularity continued to grow up until his death in 1959, at which time he was so loved by the French public that three thousand people massed outside his funeral. He had become far more than an expatriate musician; he was a national hero, with a street named in his honor.

Although the jazz cellar of the Théâtre du Vieux-Colombier has long since closed, it is still possible to see avant-garde plays at the recently refurbished theater.

Sidney Bechet at Vieux-Colombier, 1925. © Getty Images

caveau de la huchette

5 RUE DE LA HUCHETTE · PHONE: 01.43.26.65.05
WWW.CAVEAUDELAHUCHETTE.FR · OPEN DAILY: 10PM–2AM

DAMP, DARK, AND RICH WITH HISTORY, THE CAVEAU DE LA HUCHETTE IS PARIS'S OLDEST JAZZ *CAVE*. AS EARLY AS 1551 THE building was a meeting place for the Rosicrucians and the Templars, and had secret passages leading to Châtelet and the cloister of Saint-Severin. During the French Revolution, the venue was frequented by Danton, Marat, and Robespierre, who passed their nights there drinking wine and discussing politics. Later they would use the Caveau de la Huchette for trials and summary executions, earning it the nickname "Caveau de la Terreur." It is still possible to see the deep well where they disposed of incriminating evidence.

Shortly after World War II, the building was transformed into a club. It soon became a popular destination for fans of traditional jazz with an impressive roster of musicians such as Sidney Bechet, Lionel Hampton, and Memphis Slim. Today, upon descending to the bottom level, one has the feeling of having traveled fifty years into

Caveau de la Huchette, 1957. Willy Ronis © Mission du Patrinoine Photographique. Photo by: Adam Rzepka. CNAC / MNAM / Dist. Réunion des Musées Nationaux / Art Resource, NY

the past. Onstage, a band belts out traditional jazz standards, while swing dancers pack the cavernous room, furiously trying to outdo each other with the best wind-mill, octopus, daisy chain, and banana split. Some are dressed in zoot suits and print dresses; others wear the characteristic sneer of the expert swing dancer. No other club in Paris gives as good an impression of what Saint-Germain must have been like at the height of the existential movement. Prices range from 9 euros to 13 euros.

le chat quí pêche
(NOW RESTAURANT LE CHAT QUI PÉCHE)

10 RUE DE LA HUCHETTE · PHONE: 01.43.54.98.89 · MÉTRO: SAINT-MICHEL
OPEN DAILY: 11AM–3PM; 6PM–MIDNIGHT

NOW A RESTAURANT OF THE SAME NAME, LE CHAT QUI PÊCHE WAS ONCE AN ALL-NIGHT JAZZ CLUB CATERING TO SOME OF PARIS'S preeminent artists.

A small smoke-filled cellar with tiny stools, "more like instruments of torture than seats," according to Bud Powell's guardian, Francis Paudras, the club made up for its lack of charm with its soulful performers. Bud Powell graced the stage during the fifties, while Paudras, who lacked the money to attend the show, kneeled down by a grate outside and strained to listen in.

In 1964, Eric Dolphy spent long nights here jamming with the hard-bop trumpeter Donald Byrd. Like so many other jazz musicians before him, Dolphy was pleasantly surprised by the city's racial tolerance and respect for artists:

I'm on my way to Europe to live for a while. Why? Because I can get more

work there playing my own music, and because if you try to do anything different in this country, people put you down for it.

Only a month after his stint at Le Chat qui Pêche, Dolphy's expatriate dreams would be cut tragically short by his death from diabetes in Berlin.

Le Chat qui Pêche, date unknown. © Roger-Viollet

trois mailletz

56 RUE GALANDE · PHONE: 01.43.54.00.79 · MÉTRO: SAINT-MICHEL
OPEN DAILY. BAR OPENS 6PM; SHOWS START 11PM; CLUB CLOSES 5AM

THE TROIS MAILLETZ IS LOCATED IN AN ANCIENT BUILDING, WHICH WAS ONCE A RESIDENCE OF THE WORKERS WHO BUILT NOTRE-DAME. During World War II, the Resistance used the Trois Mailletz as a hideout, taking advantage of its access to Paris's vast maze of catacombs to travel through the city unseen.

One of the last of the *caves* to be constructed during the height of Saint-Germain's jazz craze, the Trois Mailletz still preserves much of the era's flavor. The *cave's* most famous regular was the trumpeter Bill Coleman, who played here on and off during the fifties. Like Sidney Bechet, Coleman had been to Paris before World War II, frequenting the bars and *boîtes* of Montmartre. When he returned in the fifties the scene had changed, and so he changed with it, settling in the newly popular Latin Quarter. In his biography, he noted: "I was so happy about being in France that I celebrated every day with a fresh bottle of cognac which I kept in my room, and I was drinking 15 to 20 cognacs in bars." Like so many jazz musicians living out of suitcases, Coleman had several bouts with alcoholism. But once he started to put down roots, his drinking abated. He met a Swiss woman whom he married and remained with for the rest of his life.

Today the Trois Mailletz is split into two levels with a piano on the first floor and nightly performances in the cellar. It is best to arrive early for shows as the tables in the cellar can fill up quickly. The music varies from jazz to blues to rock.

hotel la louísiane

60 RUE DE SEINE · PHONE: 01.44.32.17.17 · MÉTRO: MABILLON
WWW.HOTEL-LALOUISIANE.COM

URING THE FIFTIES, HOTEL LA LOUISIANE WAS THE PRIMARY RESIDENCE OF PARIS'S EXPATRIATE JAZZ COMMUNITY, HOSTING BILLIE Holiday, Miles Davis, Lester Young, and Bud Powell. According to guests at the time, the smell of red beans and fatback often wafted through the halls, while the collective sounds of saxophones, guitars, and trumpets emanated from the walls at all hours of the day. Residents would often assemble for lengthy jam sessions lasting late into the night, with everyone packing into a small dingy room to trade fours and exchange gossip about life in New York. Shortly before his death, Lester Young stayed in a room on the second floor of Hotel La Louisiane. Gravely ill, he spent most of his time drinking sweet aperitifs and dessert wines while lying in bed with his young German girlfriend.

Hotel La Louisiane was also the site of 'Round Midnight—the film based on the lives of Bud Powell and Lester Young—and a longtime residence of Bud Powell.

During his stay at the hotel, Powell was ruled by his imperious wife, Buttercup. A large and forceful woman, she kept him on high doses of tranquilizers that Francis Paudras claims dulled Powell's creativity and made him easy to manipulate. Buttercup would also often lock Powell in a room in order to prevent him from sneaking alcohol. Paudras recounts once finding Bud with one foot tied to the leg of a table while his five-year-old son ran around him in circles.

Francis Paudras was an avid fan of Bud Powell long before they met: Paudras went AWOL from his barracks in 1956 in order to see Powell perform at the Salle Pleyel. When Powell returned to France in 1959, Paudras saw him play every night at Le Chat qui Pêche until he had exhausted his savings and had to sit outside in the street and listen through a grate. It was during one of these nights that Paudras met Powell as he wandered out of the club in search of a beer. This initial encounter led to a long and deeply felt friendship which culminated in Powell living with Paudras for three years. During this time Paudras cared for the mentally unstable Powell like a son. He eased him off alcohol and harmful medication, moved into an apartment that he could hardly afford just so Powell would have room to practice, and took Powell on family vacations with his wife and child.

(I) caveau des oubliettes

52 RUE GALANDE · PHONE: 01.46.34.23.09 · MÉTRO: SAINT-MICHEL
MON–SAT: SHOWS USUALLY START AT 10PM

Once the site of the prison of Petit Châtelet, the Caveau des Oubliettes continues to play up its gruesome past with an authentic guillotine located on the ground floor. The jazz ranges from hard-bop to funk and swing, while the entry fee ranges from 4 to 7 euros.

(J) petit journal saint-michel

71 BOULEVARD SAINT-MICHEL · PHONE: 01.43.26.28.59 · MÉTRO: LUXEMBOURG
MON–SAT: SHOWS START AT 9:15PM

Dine on French cuisine while listening to traditional New Orleans jazz in this quaint club right across the street from the Jardin du Luxembourg.

RECOMMENDED LISTENING

ARMSTRONG, Louis. *Best Live convert, Vol. 1 : Jazz in Paris*. Verve.

BAKER, Josephine. *The Fabulous Josephine Baker*. RCA.

BECHET, Sidney. *From New York to Paris*. EPM Musique.

CARTER, Benny. *Further Definitions*. GRP Records.

COLEMAN, Bill. *The Great Parisian Session*. Polygram.

COLLECTION. *Swing Caraibe: Caribbean Jazz Pioneers in Paris (1929–1946)*. Frémaux and Associés.

DAVIS, Miles. *L'Ascenseur Pour L'échafaud*. Fontana.

EUROPE, James Reese. *James Reese Europe's 369th U.S. Infantry "Hellfighters" Band*. Memphis Archives.

GERSHWIN, George. *An American in Paris*. *Rhapsody in Blue*. New York Philharmonic Orchestra/Leonard Bernstein. Sony Classical.

GILLESPIE, Dizzy. *Live in Paris*. Vogue.

GRAPELLI, Stéphane. *Grappelli Story*. Verve.

HALL, Adelaide. *A Centenary Celebration*. Avid.

HAWKINS, Coleman. *Coleman Hawkins in Europe*. Timeless.

MILHAUD, Darius. *Milhaud, Poulenc, Ibert: Orchestral Works*. Ulster Orchestra/ Yan Pascal Tortelier. Chandos.

PETRUCCIANI, Michel. *Solo Live*. Dreyfus.

PORTAL, Michel. *Dockings*. Label Bleu.

PORTER, Cole. *The Very Best of Cole Porter*. Hip-O/UTV.

POWELL, Bud. *Bud Powell in Paris*. Reprise.

REINHARDT, Django. *With His American Friends*. DRG.

REINHARDT, Django and Stéphane Grappelli. *Quintette du Hot Club de France: 25 Classics 1934–1940*. ASV/Living Era.

ROMANO, Aldo. *To Be Ornette To Be*. Owl.

SATIE, Erik. *Parade/Relâche/Mercure*. New London Orchestra/Ronald Corp. Hyperion.

SOLAL, Martial. *Improvise Pour France Musique*. JMS.

TEXIER, Henri. *Izlaz*. Label Bleu.

TURNER, Joe. *Stride by Stride*. Solo Art.

CONTEMPORARY JAZZ VENUES

LE 7 LÉZARDS
10 rue des Rosiers (4th Arr.)
Genre: Jazz · Type: Club
Performances: Thurs – Sat
Phone: 01.48.87.08.97
www.7lezards.com

L'ARBUCI
25 rue de Buci (6th Arr.)
Genre: Jazz · Type: Bar/Restaurant
Performances: Wed – Sat
Phone: 01.44.32.16.00
www.arbuci.com

L'ATELIER DU PLATEAU
5 rue du Plateau (19th Arr.)
Genres: Jazz, World Music
Type: Concert Hall
Performances: Check Website
Phone: 01.42.41.28.22
www.atelierduplateau.free.fr

L'ATMOSPHERE
49 rue Lucien Sampaix (10th Arr.)
Genres: World Music, Jazz, Chanson
Française, Contemporary Music
Type: Bar · Performances: Weekends
Phone: 01.40.38.09.21

AUTOUR DE MIDI
11 rue Lepic (18th Arr.)
Genre: Jazz · Type: Club/Restaurant
Performances: Thurs – Sat
Phone: 01.55.79.16.48

BAISER SALÉ
58 rue des Lombards (1st Arr.)
Genres: Jazz Fusion, Latin Jazz,
Afro-Jazz, Blues, Rock
Type: Club/Discothèque
Performances: Daily
Phone: 01.42.33.37.71 / 06.16.54.36.87

LA BALLE AU BOND

in front of 55 quai de la Tournelle
(5th Arr.)
Genres: Jazz, Chanson Française,
Funk/Blues/Rock
Type: Bar, Concert Hall, Theater
Performances: Daily
Phone: 01.40.46.85.12
www.laballeaubond.fr

LE BATOFAR

in front of 11 quai François Mauriac
(13th Arr.)
Genres: Electro Jazz, Electronic Music, Rock
Type: Concert Hall on a Boat
Performances: Tues – Sun
Phone: 01.56.29.10.00 / 01.56.29.10.31
www.batofar.org

LE BILBOQUET

13 rue St. Benoit (6th Arr.)
Genre: Jazz
Type: Club/Discothèque/Restaurant
Performances: Daily
Phone: 01.45.48.81.84

LE BLUE NOTE

14 rue Muller (18th Arr.)
Genre: Brazilian Jazz (from Samba to
Bossa Nova to Blues) · Type: Bar
Performances: Wed – Sat
Phone: 01.42.54.69.76

LES BROCHES À L'ANCIENNE

21 rue St.-Nicolas (12th Arr.)
Genre: Jazz · Type: Club/Discothèque
Performances: Fri · Phone: 01.43.43.26.16

CAFÉ UNIVERSEL

267 rue St.-Jacques (5th Arr.)
Genres: Vocal Jazz, Latin Jazz, Bebop
Type: Café
Performances: Fri · Phone: 01.43.25.74.20

CASINO DE PARIS

16 rue de Clichy (9th Arr.)
Genres: Jazz, Musicals, Comedy
Type: Theater · Performances: Daily
Phone: 08.92.69.89.26
www.casinodeparis.fr

CAVEAU DE LA HUCHETTE
5 rue de La Huchette (5th Arr.)
Genre: Jazz · Type: Club/Discothèque
Performances: Daily
Phone: 01.43.26.65.05 / 01.43.29.52.37
www.caveaudelahuchette.fr

CAVEAU DES OUBLIETTES
52 rue Galande (5th Arr.)
Genres: Jazz, Blues, R&B
Type: Club/Discothèque
Performances: Thur – Sat
Phone: 01.44.07.06.51 / 01.46.33.60.64

THÉÂTRE DES CHAMPS-ÉLYSÉES
15 avenue Montaigne (8th Arr.)
Genres: Jazz, Classical,
Vocal Music, World Music
Type: Theater
Performances: Check Website
Phone: 01.49.52.50.50
www.theatrechampselysees.fr

LA CHAPELLE DES LOMBARDS
19 rue de Lappe (11th Arr.)
Genres: Salsa, Zouk, Reggae, Flamenco, Jazz
Type: Concert Hall
Performances: Tues – Thurs
Phone: 01.43.57.24.24 / 06.85.45.19.37

LE CITHÉA
109 rue Oberkampf
Genres : Jazz, Funk,
Latin Beats, Electronic Music
Type: Concert Hall
Performances : Check website
Phone: 01.43.57.55.13
www.cithea.com

CLUB SAINT-GERMAIN-DES-PRÉS
13 rue St.-Benoît (6th Arr.)
Genre: Jazz · Type: Bar (Upstairs)
Performances: Daily 10:30pm–2am
Phone: 01.45.48.81.84

LE DUC DES LOMBARDS

42 rue des Lombards (1st Arr.)
Genre: Jazz · Type: Club
Performances: Daily
Phone: 01.42.33.22.88

ÉLYSÉE MONTMARTRE

72 bd Rochechouart (18th Arr.)
Genres: All Types
Type: Concert Hall
Performances: Check Website
Phone: 01.44.92.45.36
www.elyseemontmartre.com

LE FRANC PINOT

1 quai Bourbon (4th Arr.)
Genre: Jazz · Type: Club/Restaurant
Performances:
Piano & Vocal Jazz Tues – Thurs
Concerts Fri & Sat
Phone: 01.46.33.60.64

GLAZ'ART

7/15 av. de la Porte de la Villette
(19th Arr.)
Genres: Rock, Electronic,
World, Jazz, Chanson Française
Type: Concert Hall
Performances: Daily
Phone: 01.40.36.55.65
www.glazart.com

HOUDON JAZZ BAR

5 rue des Abbesses (18th Arr.)
Genre: Jazz · Type: Bar
Performances: Fri & Sat
Phone: 01.46.06.35.91

JAZZ CLUB LIONEL HAMPTON

Hotel Méridien Étoile, 81 bd Gouvion St.-Cyr
(17th Arr.)
Genres: Jazz, Blues, Soul · Type: Club
Performances: Daily
Phone: 01.40.68.30.42
www.lemeridien-paris.com

LA MAROQUINERIE

23 rue Boyer (20th Arr.)
Genres: All Kinds
Type: Concert Hall
Performances: Check Website
Phone: 01.40.33.30.60
www.lamaroquinerie.fr

NEW MORNING

7/9 rue des Petites Ecuries (10th Arr.)
Genres: Jazz, World Music, Funk, Salsa
Type: Concert Hall
Performances: Tues – Sat
Phone: 01.45.23.56.39
www.newmorning.com

THÉÂTRE DE L'OLYMPIA BRUNO COQUATRIX

28 bd des Capucines (9th Arr.)
Genres: All Kinds
Type: Concert Hall
Performances: Daily
Phone 01.47.41.25.49
www.olympiahall.com

OPUS JAZZ AND SOUL CLUB

167 quai de Valmy (10th Arr.)
Genres: Jazz, Gospel, Funk,
Soul, Oriental Latino, R&B
Types: Bar/Restaurant/Concert Hall
Performances: Tues – Sun
Phone: 01.40.34.70.00

PARIS-PRAGUE JAZZ CLUB

Centre Tchèque, 18 rue Bonaparte
(6th Arr.)
Genre: Jazz · Type: Club
Performances: Fri
Phone: 01.53.73.00.22
www.centretcheque.org

PENICHE BLUES CAFÉ

Port de la Gare (13th Arr.)
Genres: All Styles
Type: Concert Hall/Bar
Performances: Daily except
Mon & Wed
Phone: 01.45.84.24.88

LE PETIT JOURNAL MONTPARNASSE

13 rue du Commandant Mouchotte
(14th Arr.)
Genre: Jazz · Type: Bar
Performances: Daily except Sun
Phone: 01.43.21.56.70
www.petitjournal-montparnasse.com

PETIT JOURNAL ST.-MICHEL

71 bd St.-Michel (5th Arr.)
Genre: Traditional Jazz · Type: Bar
Performances: Daily except Sun
Phone: 01.43.26.28.59

QUAI DU BLUES

17 bd Vital-Bouhot
(just north of 17th Arr.)
Neuilly - Île De Jatte
Genres: Blues, Gospel, Soul, R&B
Type: Club
Performances: Thur − Sat
Phone : 01.46.24.22.00
www.quaidublues.com

SALLE PLEYEL

252 rue du Faubourg-St.-Honoré
(8th Arr.)
Genres: Jazz, Classical
Type: Concert Hall
Performances: Schedule varies
Phone: 01.45.61.53.00

SLOW CLUB

130 rue de Rivoli (1st Arr.)
Genres: Jazz, Rock;
Hiphop on Sunday Nights
Type: Club
Performances: Daily except Mon & Wed
Phone: 01.42.33.84.30

STUDIO DES ISLETTES

10 rue des Islettes (18th Arr.)
Genre: Jazz · Type: Club
Performances: Fri & Sat
Phone: 01.42.58.63.33
www.studiodesislettes.com

SUNSET / SUNSIDE

60 rue des Lombards (1st Arr.)
Genres: Electric Jazz,
Electro/World Music, Vocal Jazz
Type: Club
Performances: Mon – Sat
Phone: 01.40.26.46.60 / 01.40.26.21.25

TROIS MAILLETZ

56 rue Galande (5th Arr.)
Genres: Jazz, Blues, Rock
Type: Bar upstairs, cellar downstairs
Performances: Daily, Bar Opens 6pm;
Shows Start 11pm
Phone: 01.43.54.00.79

UTOPIA

79 rue de l'Ouest (14th Arr.)
Genres: Blues, R&B, Country
Type: Club
Performances: Daily
Phone: 01.43.22.79.66

SELECTED BIBLIOGRAPHY

Baker, Jean-Claude with Chris Chase. *Josephine: The Hungry Heart*. Random House, 1993.

Balmer, Paul. *Stéphane Grappelli: With and Without Django*. Sanctuary Publishing, 2003.

Berger, Morroe, Edward Berger, and James Patrick. *Benny Carter: A Life in American Music*. Scarecrow Press, 2002.

Bergreen, Laurence. *Louis Armstrong*. Broadway, 1998.

Blake, Jody. *Le Tumulte Noir: Modernist Art and Popular Entertainment in Jazz-Age Paris, 1900–1930*. Pennsylvania State University Press, 1999.

Bricktop with James Haskins. *Bricktop*. Atheneum, 1983.

Brierre, Jean-Dominique. *Le Jazz français de 1900 à Aujourd'hui*. Hors Collection, 2000.

Carr, Ian. *Miles Davis: The Definitive Biography*. Thunder's Mouth Press, 1999.

Castarède, Jean. *Moulin Rouge*. Empire, 2001.

Chilton, John. *Sidney Bechet: The Wizard of Jazz*. Da Capo Press, 1996.

Chilton, John. *The Song of the Hawk: The Life and Recordings of Coleman Hawkins*. University of Michigan Press, 1990.

Davis, Miles with Quincy Troupe. *Miles: The Autobiography*. Simon and Schuster, 1989.

Delaunay, Charles, translated by Michael James. *Django Reinhardt*. Da Capo Press, 1981.

Delaunay, Luc, translated by Elena B. Odio. *Pres: The Story of Lester Young*. University of Arkansas Press, 1993.

Goddard, Chris. *Jazz Away from Home*. Paddington Press, 1979.

Hennessey, Mike. *Klook: The Story of Kenny Clarke*. Quartet Books, 1990.

Hyland, William G. *George Gershwin: A New Biography*. Praeger Publishers, 2003.

Lloyd, Craig. *Eugene Bullard: Black Expatriate in Jazz-Age Paris*. University of Georgia Press, 2000.

Martin, Denis-Constant and Olivier Roueff. *La France du jazz: Musique Modernité et Identité dans la Première Moitié du XXe Siècle*. Parenthèses, 2000.

McBrien, William. *Cole Porter: A Biography*. Alfred A. Knopf, 1998.

Moody, Bill. *The Jazz Exiles: American Musicians Abroad*. University of Nevada Press, 1993.

Paudras, Francis, translated by Rubye Monet, English translation edited by Warren Bernhardt. *Dance of the Infidels: A Portrait of Bud Powell*. Da Capo Press, 1998.

Rey, Anne. *Satie*. Seuil, 1995.

Roy, Jean. *Le Groupe des Six*. Seuil, 1994.

Steegmuller, Francis. *Cocteau: A Biography*. David R. Godine, 1992.

Stovall, Tyler. *Paris Noir: African Americans in the City of Light*. Houghton Mifflin, 1996.

Tournès-Fortin, Ludovic. *New Orleans sur Seine: L'Aventure du Jazz en France (1917–1992)*. Fayard, 1999.

Vian, Boris. *Manuel de Saint-Germain-des-Prés*. LGF–Livre de Poche, 2000.

Shack, William A. *Harlem in Montmartre: A Paris Jazz Story Between the Great Wars*. University of California Press, 2001.

Williams, Iain Cameron. *Underneath a Harlem Moon: The Harlem to Paris Years of Adelaide Hall*. Continuum, 2002.

ABOUT THE AUTHOR

Following his graduation from Stanford University, Luke Miner worked at *The New York Review of Books* and later received a degree from the École des Hautes Études en Sciences Sociales. He now lives in Paris, where he works as a freelance writer.

The author would like to thank Jessica Powell, Nadia Aguiar, Angela Hederman, and Julia Holmes for all of their help.